Butch

Trading with Candlesticks

Trading with Candlesticks

Visual Tools for Improved
Technical Analysis and Timing

Michael C. Thomsett

Vice President, Publisher: Tim Moore
Associate Publisher and Director of Marketing: Amy Neidlinger
Executive Editor: Jim Boyd
Editorial Assistant: Pamela Boland
Operations Manager: Gina Kanouse
Senior Marketing Manager: Julie Phifer
Publicity Manager: Laura Czaja
Assistant Marketing Manager: Megan Colvin
Cover Designer: Alan Clements
Managing Editor: Kristy Hart
Project Editor: Anne Goebel
Copy Editor: Chuck Hutchinson
Proofreader: Kathy Ruiz
Senior Compositor: Gloria Schurick
Manufacturing Buyer: Dan Uhrig

© 2011 by Pearson Education, Inc.
Publishing as FT Press
Upper Saddle River, New Jersey 07458

This book is sold with the understanding that neither the author nor the publisher is engaged in rendering legal, accounting, or other professional services or advice by publishing this book. Each individual situation is unique. Thus, if legal or financial advice or other expert assistance is required in a specific situation, the services of a competent professional should be sought to ensure that the situation has been evaluated carefully and appropriately. The author and the publisher disclaim any liability, loss, or risk resulting directly or indirectly, from the use or application of any of the contents of this book.

FT Press offers excellent discounts on this book when ordered in quantity for bulk purchases or special sales. For more information, please contact U.S. Corporate and Government Sales, 1-800-382-3419, corpsales@pearsontechgroup.com. For sales outside the U.S., please contact International Sales at international@pearson.com.

Company and product names mentioned herein are the trademarks or registered trademarks of their respective owners.

All rights reserved. No part of this book may be reproduced, in any form or by any means, without permission in writing from the publisher.

Printed in the United States of America

First Printing August 2010
ISBN-10: 0-13-138094-X
ISBN-13: 978-0-13-138094-3
Pearson Education LTD.
Pearson Education Australia PTY, Limited
Pearson Education Singapore, Pte. Ltd.
Pearson Education North Asia, Ltd.
Pearson Education Canada, Ltd.
Pearson Educatión de Mexico, S.A. de C.V.
Pearson Education—Japan
Pearson Education Malaysia, Pte. Ltd.

Library of Congress Cataloging-in-Publication Data:
Thomsett, Michael C.
  Trading with candlesticks : visual tools for improved technical analysis and timing / Michael C. Thomsett.
      p. cm.
  Includes index.
  ISBN-13: 978-0-13-138094-3 (hardback : alk. paper)
  ISBN-10: 0-13-138094-X
  1. Stocks—Charts, diagrams, etc. 2. Investment analysis. 3. Portfolio management. I. Title.
  HG4638.T46 2011
  332.63'2042—dc22
                                                2010010281

Contents

Acknowledgments viii
About the Author ix
Introduction 1

Chapter 1 **The Basic Candlestick** 5
The Origin and Meaning of the Candlestick 6
Strengths and Weaknesses of Candlesticks 9
Paper Trading as a Testing Ground 12
The Skills Every Trader Needs 14
Candlesticks: General Observations Concerning Their Use 18
Expanding the Information Pool Effectively 20
Endnotes 22

Chapter 2 **Single-Stick Signs** 25
Uptrends and Downtrends 25
The Significance of a Candlestick's Shape 28
Variations on the Bullish Long Candlestick 30
The Mistake Pattern 32
The Spinning Top, Hanging Man, and Hammer 37
The Significance of Tails 42

Chapter 3 **Double-Stick Moves** 47
Two Reversal Moves: Engulfing and Harami 48
More Reversals: The Inverted Hammer and Doji Star 53
Even More Reversals: Meeting Lines and Piercing Lines 56
Confirming Patterns: Thrusting, Separating, and Neck Lines 60
Reversal and Confirming Moves—Relative Values 66

Chapter 4	**Complex Stick Patterns** **69**
	Reversal Trend Change Patterns 71
	Reversal Trend Inside and Outside Formations 74
	Reversal Stars and Abandoned Babies 78
	Complex Trend Patterns 82
	Complex Gap Trends 86
Chapter 5	**Reversal Pattern Analysis** **91**
	Recognizing the Bull Reversal 91
	Recognizing the Bear Reversal 94
	The Doji as a Reversal Signal 97
	Reversal Patterns with Gaps 101
	Reversals Setting New Support or Resistance 104
	More Resistance and Support Reversals 108
	Multisession Gap Reversals 111
Chapter 6	**Volume and Volatility** **119**
	Volume as a Price Indicator 119
	Volume Indicators 122
	Volume Indicators and Candlesticks 126
	Testing Price Volatility 131
Chapter 7	**Buy and Sell Setup Signals** **141**
	Price Spikes and Reaction Swings 143
	Percentage Swing Systems 146
	Short-Term Gapping Behavior 149
	Anticipating the Trend During Consolidation 153
	The Setup Pattern and Swing 156
	Support and Resistance in the Swing Trade 165
Chapter 8	**Swing Trading with Candlesticks** **171**
	A Swing Trading Overview 171
	Quantifying Price Movement with Candlesticks 174
	The Importance of Convergence and Divergence 178
	Primary Trends and Candlestick-Based Entry or Exit 182
	Setup Criteria and Action Points 186
	Selling Short in Swing Trades 190

Chapter 9 Spotting Trends and Using Trendlines **193**
    Identifying the Trendline 194
    Trendlines and Candlesticks as Confirmation 200
    Applying Moving Averages to Candlestick Analysis 203

Chapter 10 Technical Indicators **207**
    The Value of Confirmation 207
    A Review: Technical Analysis Basics 209
    The Significance of Gaps 212
    A Key Framework: Support and Resistance 215
    Overbought and Oversold Indicators 217
    The Potential of Candlestick Signals 222

Glossary **225**

Index **235**

Acknowledgments

Thanks to the many options industry folks who have shared information generously and provided support for this and many other projects, especially stockcharts.com, whose generous permissions policy has helped bring this topic to life. I also want to thank Tina Logan, author of *Getting Started in Candlestick Charting* (John Wiley & Sons, 2008) for her willingness to help me, as a competitor, in the early stages of developing this book.

Special thanks go to Jim Boyd of FT Press who, as executive editor, provided editorial guidance and support of this project, and to the excellent editorial and production staff working with him.

About the Author

Michael C. Thomsett has authored dozens of financial books. These include *Options Trading for the Conservative Investor* (FT Press); *Winning with Options* (Amacom Books); *The LEAPS Strategist* (Marketplace Books); and the best-selling *Getting Started in Options* (John Wiley & Sons), now in its 8th edition with over 250,000 copies sold.

Thomsett is also author of *The Investment and Securities Dictionary* (McFarland), named by *Choice Magazine* as an Outstanding Academic Book for 1988, and many other investment and trading books. Before starting his professional writing career in 1978, Thomsett was an accountant. He also spent seven years as a consultant in the financial services industry with clients including securities broker/dealers, insurance master agencies, and insurance companies. He has been an active options trader since the mid-1970s.

Thomsett lives in Nashville, Tennessee, and writes full time.

Introduction

Confusion and uncertainty: the two common attributes of the stock market. The random short-term movements in public trading create a lot of confusion and certainly add to uncertainty among traders. A novice understands this reality, but even experienced professionals who have been trading for years suffer the same affliction.

This is where chart analysis becomes valuable. No one can claim a perfect record of timing buy and sell decisions, and no one realistically expects to beat the market with every trade. It is enough to beat the averages and to outperform the typical profit or loss experience ratio. For many, today's profits are eroded by tomorrow's losses, and so many individual traders find themselves seeking trades just to get back up to dead even. The candlestick chart is a valuable tool that helps you anticipate trends in a stock's price and improve the timing of buy and sell orders. Ironically, even experienced traders who refer regularly to candlestick charts often are not well versed in recognition of patterns or their significance.

This book first describes candlestick charts in detail and shows how they are constructed. The advantage with this visual aid is that you can find all the price information in one symbol. This includes a day's opening and closing price, the trading range, and direction (upward or downward) of movement. The candlestick also shows each day's *breadth* of trading range. When you view an array of charts over a number of trading periods, you can determine in an instant whether a stock is high- or low-volatility, whether it is trending upward or downward, and most of all, *when* to make a move. Collectively, this is a valuable set of statistics. Most traders who have analyzed price movement using candlesticks understand these basic attributes, but if this is the extent of your understanding, you need more.

Beyond the basics, this book explains how to recognize different kinds of signs, moves, and patterns (bull, bear, reversal, and market) and how to employ double and triple stick formations to better understand why prices are behaving in a particular manner. Many of these moves and patterns are subtle, and their meaning is easily lost in the more recognizable patterns most traders seek.

Candlesticks are also valuable when analyzed in combination with other indicators. For example, two factors often overlooked in price-focused technical analysis are the critical attributes of price movement and risk: volume and volatility. This book explains how candlestick chart analysis employing these important features will help you improve your mastery of stock trading. Advanced technical analysis can be greatly enhanced by combining candlestick indicators with the better-known price patterns and trends.

Chapter 7, "Buy and Sell Setup Signals," examines and analyzes the use of swing trading techniques to improve the timing of trades. A setup is a sign found in candlestick movement and breadth, pointing to the best timing of either buy or sell, and also serving as a confirmation tool. Adding to this the trend indicators found in moving averages, you gain valuable insights that will become indispensable in your daily trading strategy. Moving averages show you not only where prices are today, but how these are significant in terms of what will happen next. Unfortunately, the popular convergence signals often come too late to take action and maximize the timing advantage. This is where candlestick patterns can help you anticipate trends well before other indicators solidify the information.

The entire range of technical indicators involves timing of decisions. Candlestick charts are timing tools not only for trends in upward or downward directions, but also for determining the strength of the current movement or its weakness. Some patterns are easily identified, whereas others reflect a lot of uncertainty among traders. The endless struggle between buyers and sellers usually involves one side or the other dominating the price movement, but at times buyers and sellers are deadlocked. This condition is just as important as a strong bull or bear pattern because it also helps time your decision to buy, sell, or take no action.

After introducing the patterns of single and combined candlesticks, exploring setup signals, and examining moving averages, *Trading with Candlesticks* concludes with an analysis of candlesticks used in combination with technical indicators that most chart analysts employ. Analysis of price movement requires at least a rudimentary appreciation of a few very important price patterns, and these are most readily recognized with candlestick patterns. Whether you are an active day trader, a swing trader, or a technician, this book provides the essential visual and interpretative information you need to expand your technical knowledge. Even the conservative value investor who dabbles in speculation from time to time will find great value in the study of candlestick charts.

The book combines several important features to help you. They include sidebars with key points and definitions, ample checklists, and examples and charts of actual companies demonstrating candlestick chart movement and their interpretation. A word about the charts of actual companies: No matter which company's charts are used or when they are picked, any chart is likely to reflect a range of prices that is out of date by the time this book is published. Most of the charts in this book are from familiar Blue Chip companies because these names are well known to most people, and that familiarity makes the analysis more accessible and practical for most readers. Remember, though, that even an out-of-date chart is revealing. It's not the price level or current condition of a stock that matters, but the pattern and strength or weakness of price movement. The observations based on these charts apply to all stocks and at all price levels.

The charts are also consistent in their time frame. They are mostly one-month daily summaries of price movement. This approach was selected because a majority of traders think in terms of the opening and closing price, breadth of trading, and direction on a *daily* basis. Stocks open and close within the easily defined day, and this is the best-known trading period. But it is also important to understand that chartists use a variety of different trading periods—hourly, 15-minute, or 5-minute charts, for example. The amazing thing about charting is that no matter what length of time you use in your chart analysis, the same rules and observations apply. A pattern is going to be found in a daily or weekly chart and likewise in a one-minute chart. The significance of movement is identical even though the timing of trade decisions is different. So a trader oriented to making decisions from day to day is going to act in the venue of "daily" change. A day trader, in comparison, is likely to use the shorter-term charts and make decisions in terms of hours or even minutes. Both are using the same trading information, moving averages, and patterns; that is the fact worth remembering.

Finally, the question must arise: Where do you find free charts? Many Web sites offer free charts for virtually any listed stock, and you can use these sites to get what you need for stocks you want to track and trade. These sites also offer subscriptions that include more advanced features beyond the basic delayed-quote chart. For many traders, the free information provided by brokerage firms, financial companies, and others is enough. For other traders, the cost of a subscription makes the added information worth the price.

This book is intended for the experienced trader and technician who wants to find out how charting can improve technical analysis or who needs to add to a body of knowledge about interpreting technical patterns and time buy, sell, and hold decisions. Candlesticks are one of the best tools for aiding analysis of stock prices and confirming indicated reversals and continuations or, equally important, spotting signals that are going to fail. The point of adding to technical knowledge through confirmation signals is to improve timing and to employ more traditional technical indicators in an effective timing strategy.

chapter 1

The Basic Candlestick

Candlestick charting combines all the needed features of daily stock movement: opening and closing, breadth of the day's trading, upward or downward price movement, and high/low prices reached during the day. This is achieved through a combination of shape and color.

📖 Candlestick Chart

A visual summary of all the trading action in a single period, showing the opening and closing prices, breadth of trading, and upward or downward movement in price.

At the same time, candlesticks are easy to understand. They are actually quite simple in what they reveal. If you had to construct your own candlestick chart for a single day, it would not take very long, although building a 30-day chart would be quite an undertaking. Fortunately, modern technology includes numerous free Internet sites that provide candlestick charts in an instant, for any period you want to review, and with any combination of indicators (price only, volume, moving averages, MACD, and RSI, for example). The range of information is explained in greater detail in coming chapters. For now, you need to be sure you understand the basics of candlesticks so that you can maximize them.

The Origin and Meaning of the Candlestick

Why it is called a "candlestick"? The answer is its shape—a vertical rectangle with a smaller "wick" on the top and on the bottom. All these shapes have great significance, of course. The use of this valuable visual tool is traced to Japan in the seventeenth century. The Dojima Rice Exchange in Osaka traded mainly in rice during that period, and the use of futures contracts became necessary. As the world's first futures exchange anywhere, traders on the Dojima developed the candlestick as a way to track futures contract trends.

> ✓ **Key Point**
>
> *A candlestick is a highly visual representation of price history, showing each period's opening and closing price, the trading range, and price direction.*

📖 Trend

The direction of price movement over time, which continues in the same direction until it weakens and moves sideways or reverses.

    The futures contract—whether for rice or any other commodity—is a market necessity. When farmers plant their crops, they need to know in advance that there will be a market for their product, even though it won't exist for several months. Without knowing whether there is a market, the farmers cannot know how much to plant. The futures contract is a commitment from end users (retail merchants and others who need the rice product in later months). It guarantees a price based on market conditions at the moment. As those conditions change, the value of the futures contract changes as well. With growth in demand, the futures contract rises, and if demand falls, so does the futures price. For the farmers, buying a futures contract locks in a price. When the product goes to market, they can sell for the market price (if higher) or if the market has fallen, they can sell their futures contract and get the price they need.

    Just as stock prices rise or fall for any number of reasons, commodity prices are also affected by factors no one can anticipate. This explains why it is so important for growers to be able to lock in a minimum price. A large-scale crop failure means less rice and much greater prices, for example. With this in mind, end users are also interested in locking in the price they have to pay, so both sellers (farmers) and buyers can take advantage of futures contracts to add certainty to the market.

This is where candlesticks enter the picture.

In Japan by the eighteenth century, the rice trade was extensive, involving not only the trade between local growers and consumers, but international commerce as well. Analysts in Japan noticed that several factors affected futures prices. They included weather patterns as well as the tendencies among traders to act in a particular way based on market conditions. Today, stock market wisdom is based on the same trends. When prices rise, traders tend to become greedy and overbuy, and when prices fall, they tend to panic and sell. So the act of buying high and selling low is more common than the advice to buy low and sell high. The two factors at work—greed and panic—lead many traders to take the wrong actions based on market conditions. Traders use the candlestick to improve their timing for both buying and selling positions, based not on gut reaction or emotion, but on recognizable trend patterns. The candlestick is a valuable tool because it makes it so easy to recognize those patterns.

As a charting tool, the candlestick reveals much more than the traditional bar chart, also called the OHLC (open, high, low, close). The OHLC is easy to construct, but with online free charting services, the more complex and revealing candlestick chart makes much more sense.

OHLC Chart

Abbreviation of "open, high, low, close." A type of stock chart showing a vertical stick for the day's trading range and two vertical, shorter protrusions showing opening and closing prices.

Trading Range

The price spread between highest and lowest points on a daily bar or over a period of time; the breadth of trading between those two points.

If you had to build your own charts every day, the OHLC chart would be easier to work with than the candlestick. But with the free Internet services available, you can use candlesticks to get much better visual summaries for the same effort. A side-by-side view of both chart types makes this point. Figure 1-1 compares OHLC and candlestick charts for the same price movement of a stock.

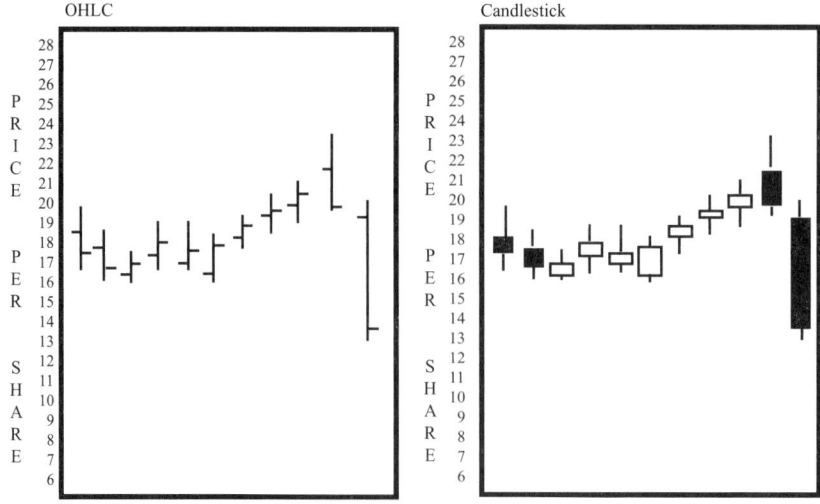

Figure 1-1 Comparison of OHLC and candlestick charts

Notice how much more information you see—instantly—with the candlestick chart. The first two and last two days are downward-moving (black boxes), and all the rest are upward-moving (white boxes). The extensions above and below the boxes show the trading range, whereas the opening and closing prices are found on the top and bottom of the box. When the trend is downward, the top of the box is the opening price and the bottom is the closing price, and vice versa for an uptrend day.

Each attribute of the candlestick has a name. Figure 1-2 summarizes the names of each segment of the candlestick.

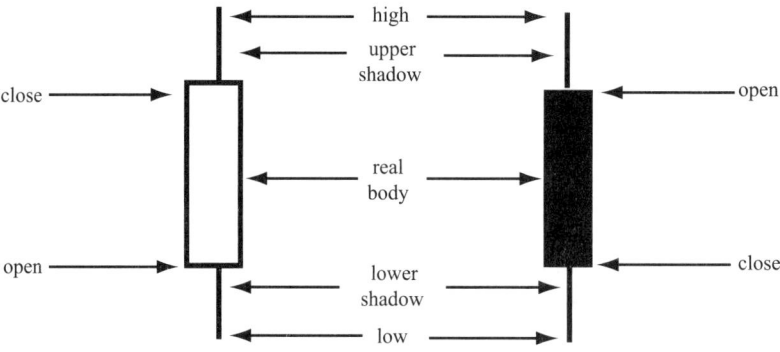

Figure 1-2 The candlestick

> ✓ **Key Point**
>
> The white candlestick occurs when prices move up, and a black rectangle occurs when prices move down. This makes it easy to see, at a glance, the direction and duration of every trend.

The open and close are opposite on upward- and downward-trending days, as Figure 1-2 shows. The rectangular box (the real body) is the range from the day's opening to closing price. The full breadth of trading, including extensions above and below the range of open-to-close, is represented by the upper and lower shadows. When you compare the candlestick to the same day's OHLC, the candlestick's advantages are clear. It is more visually revealing, especially when you view a series of days next to one another.

📖 Real Body

The rectangle in a candlestick, representing the area between the day's opening and closing price but excluding the total range above and below those levels (upper and lower shadows).

📖 Shadow

The portion of the candlestick above and below the real body. The upper shadow shows the distance between the trading range (open to close) and the highest price of the day, and the lower shadow shows the distance between the trading range and the lowest price of the day.

Strengths and Weaknesses of Candlesticks

The most apparent benefit of candlesticks is their immediate revelation of trends. The first illustration (Figure 1-1) showed this by comparison. The uptrend (white bodies) and downtrend (black bodies) days jumped out of the formation. As with most types of analysis, no single day's results are as important as the multiday trend, and this is where candlesticks present a definite advantage.

With the OHLC chart, the movement is tracked over a period of time, but it is much more difficult to recognize a trend. In the next few chapters, you will discover how bull and bear trends, reversal and market patterns all develop, and are recognizable with candlesticks. The greatest advantage is going to be found in what is revealed in double-stick and triple-stick patterns. These are two-day and three-day formations that foreshadow movement and provide indications of the strength (or weakness) in the current trend.

This is the primary advantage to candlesticks. Because all the price information is represented in a visual format involving side and color, the importance of the trend as it evolves is more readily seen. This improves your timing for entering and exiting positions. The simple formation of the candlestick gives you a lot of information in a split-second glance.

Traders like to know as quickly as possible whether the short-term trend is bullish (white) or bearish (black). With the OHLC chart, the implications of day-to-day change are not as obvious, so the trend is also more difficult to spot, not only in terms of direction, but also in terms of strength or weakness. As a trend evolves, the strength or weakness is likely to change as well, and the candlestick is the most effective tool for recognizing this change.

For review over a long period of time, candlesticks are more limited than the OHLC chart. Because the candlestick is wider than the simple OHLC stick, a chart with a longer time period gets crowded with candlesticks. To solve this problem, traders may abandon the daily chart format in favor of weekly summaries. This approach simplifies the chart but may combine information in a way that obscures the detailed trend as well as meaningful patterns as they emerge. Most traders need to study every day's price movement to better understand both price behavior and trader opinions. The use of longer periods makes chart reviews easier but obscures the important daily trend. A solution is to limit chart duration (for example, reviewing no more than one month at a time) and use separate charts to study longer-term trends. When charts with the same scale are placed side by side, multiple months can be reviewed without the confusion resulting from overcrowding of the candlestick bodies.

Another drawback to candlesticks is that trends can be misinterpreted if the chart itself is not studied carefully. False and failing signals are common in all forms of charting, so everyone relying on the timing provided in charts has to proceed with caution. A series of uptrend days, for example, might indicate a bullish condition in the stock. But if the trading range or the range between high and low is narrowing, the field of white charts could easily obscure a more revealing internal development in the price trend. A continuing uptrend may be weakening, in fact, so the attributes of the candlestick have to be reviewed in full context, and not just by color of the real body.

Candlesticks, like all charts, are restricted to price trends and, in some cases, to volume in the stock. This means that technical data beyond the daily trading range and price direction may be ignored in the analysis. If you want to develop a complete view of the current trend, you also need moving averages and other technical data to make the review as complete as possible. The judgment you bring to the timing of trades requires consideration of many attributes, not just the short-term price trend. Although traders do tend to make decisions based on short-term price changes, the intermediate and long-term trends are equally important. This is where it becomes valuable to combine candlestick analysis with moving averages and a few other revealing technical indicators. Fortunately, many free charting sites provide this additional information as part of the complete chart.

✓ Key Point

No single indicator is valuable unless viewed in a larger context. Candlestick charts show the greatest insight when the sticks are augmented with moving averages and other technical data.

Candlesticks are valuable, but by themselves, they do not give you the entire story. As you move through the book, additional indicators and their confirmation value will be introduced one by one and explained. By the end of the book, you will see how bringing a full range of technical signals into your analysis enriches your analytical capabilities. Based on the candlestick as a primary initial indicator, you will also know how to employ volume, moving averages, and a few other important technical gauges.

With any form of charting—whether OHLC or candlesticks—improving the instances of well-timed decisions is in itself a worthwhile outcome. Experienced traders know that not every trade will be profitable or well timed, and that each poorly timed trade is a learning experience. This is why diversification is so crucial for successful trading. Candlesticks are valuable tools for developing a body of informed knowledge, but no analytical tool can ensure 100 percent profitability.

With candlestick analysis, as with most forms of technical study, you need to master a large number of patterns and come to understand their significance, apply these patterns to actual situations, and evaluate outcomes. These steps help you not only to develop working knowledge of candlestick chart analysis, but also to find out what can go wrong. This knowledge—the negative or loss experience—is at least as valuable as having a series of trades that are all profitable. Losing is also an experience, but one that is more painful than what you learn through winning.

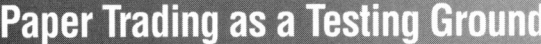
Paper Trading as a Testing Ground

Improving technical expertise by employing a paper trading program makes sense. This is a trial run for a portfolio, in which you start out with a fictitious portfolio, enter buy and sell orders, and see the resulting profits and losses. Because you are improving your observations while going through these paper trades, you do not actually lose money, but you can discover how trades are likely to come out and how analysis of candlesticks improves what you already know how to do. So reliance on a chart pattern that is not as reliable as you had thought is very instructive. Paper trading helps you to better appreciate the subtle meaning of patterns and how information can be misread. For any system, paper trading is a smart technique. Even experienced traders can benefit by trying out expansions on a technical program in a paper trading forum, before putting real money on the line. You might benefit by maintaining a paper trading system alongside your "real money" portfolio.

📖 Paper Trading

A method for becoming familiar with strategies, in which a fictitious portfolio is traded using "virtual money." This technique enables you to see the outcomes of different timing strategies, but without losing real money.

Many sites offer free paper trading software, many promoted as contests or games (with prizes awarded for the best-performing paper portfolio), and others are simply free initially, leading to promotions for membership in more advanced services. Many brokerage firms offer variations of this idea; the following sites also offer free paper trading programs:

- *Investopedia* link to Investopedia's Investing Game at www.investopedia.com
- *Trading Simulation* link to Virtual Paper Trading at www.tradingsimulation.com
- *Wall Street Survivor* link to Virtual Stock and Option Portfolio at www.wallstreetsurvivor.com
- *Market Watch* link to Virtual Stock Exchange at http://vse.marketwatch.com
- *How the Market Works* link to Fantasy Stock Trading at www.howthemarketworks.com

- *Virtual Stock Trading* link to Virtual Stock Trading Games at www.virtualstocktrading.com
- *UMOO* link to Tournament Lobby at www.umoo.com

Of course, all Web sites offering free features also promote sponsored subscription services or try to sell upgrades to you. These sites are useful for starting out in a paper trading program, though, and they provide opportunities for you to apply what you learn about candlestick charts as you move through the learning process.

> ✓ **Key Point**
>
> *Paper trading is a method for making simulated trades without risking capital. This activity aids in improving your analytical and timing skills.*

The most valuable insight you can expect from a paper trading program as an ongoing technical management process is to seek a correlation between your interpretations of candlestick patterns with actual price behavior. This involves two aspects. First, economic factors are involved, which are complex and far reaching but can be summed up and described as the forces of "supply and demand." Most traders know how this works: increased demand for stock drives up the price, and weakening demand drives down the price. This involves far more than market forces in their pure form, however; outside economic news, earnings, competition, consumer confidence, cyclical changes, and much more also provide change to prices in both directions. It's the second factor that is more interesting and subtle: the trading behavior of "the market" as a collection of investors. Much of the daily price movement of stocks is chaotic and represents overreaction to news and information. Swing traders know this and trade on the emotions of the market. Whether you are swing trading or using candlesticks as confirmation tools, being aware of how short-term price movement works greatly improves your timing. By resisting the urge to jump onto the emotional roller coaster of the market, you are able to look for patterns as they emerge and improve your short-term entry and exit strategies.

Detailed tracking of candlestick charts for a particular stock reveals how prices change based on current news and financial reports. It is interesting to see how different stocks react to the same news; for example, if one company's quarterly earnings report is below expectations, that company's competitors might see a temporary upward movement in the stock price. If a national statistic is promising, stocks in affected sectors will react positively (or when the statistic is negative, the same stock prices might fall).

None of the short-term cause and effect in stock price movement is meaningful in the long term. Value investing calls for holding onto shares for months or years. However, that short-term price movement is where you find trading opportunities. By tracking stock price changes through candlestick charts (along with other technical indicators), you discover patterns that signal the time to make a move. These are most often based not on long-term fundamental value, but more on what is taking place today and tomorrow.

You are going to discover that there are two major areas to focus on in the use of candlesticks within your technical program. First is the tendency for the stock to react to market news; some stocks react with volatile price changes to even the slightest change, whereas other stocks tend to ignore news. The second area to focus on is the development of chart patterns and trends. This is where most chart watchers focus, but you need to study both the stock's reaction to market news and the development of chart patterns.

The Skills Every Trader Needs

Anyone embarking on a new strategy has to accept the learning curve that goes with it. Even experienced traders who will be analyzing stocks based on candlestick formations for the first time have to proceed cautiously. There are five important skills every trader needs, based on experience as well as your personal risk tolerance. Every trader needs to review his strategies and portfolio continuously even after years of experience, to make sure he is not violating his own trading rules (specifically, goals set based on risk tolerance and market conditions).

Risk Tolerance

The degree of risk you are willing and able to take in your portfolio, based on many factors including knowledge about the market, experience, capital, budget, portfolio size, and personal financial situation. The defined risk tolerance level identifies the kinds of investments anyone can afford to make.

> ✓ **Key Point**
> Knowing how much risk to take is critical for every investor; equally important is mastering analytical tools like candlesticks to ensure that you can use them most effectively.

These five important skills are

1. *A complete appreciation of the risk element in all trading.* Everyone knows that risk, as a general concept, is the chance of losing money instead of making money. But in fact, risk has numerous other aspects that everyone needs to know about. These aspect include the double exposure to taxes and inflation, for example. You need to know your breakeven rate, the rate you need to earn *net* of taxes, to match inflation and break even.[1]

   Many of these risks (like the tax and inflation risk) are invisible. For example, you might be exposed to an invisible risk if you have diversified your portfolio into many different stocks and sectors, all of which are exposed to the same economic or cyclical effects. To determine whether or not you are adequately situated based on your own risk tolerance level, you need to evaluate a range of different risk-related questions.

2. *The ability to **effectively** diversify without going too far.* The concept of diversification is more complicated than some traders realize. It is not enough to own several different stocks if they are in the same market sector, or are subject to similar or identical market forces. Diversification can take many forms, including division between direct stock and mutual fund shares; equity and debt; nonstock trading in futures, options or ETF[2] shares; and using hedging strategies to reduce risks (for example, offsetting stocks with gold or currency positions).

   At the same time, there is another danger: overdiversification. If you spread capital around too much, you can gain only the average rate of the entire portfolio. This could mean your potential profits are reduced because strong positions are absorbed by weaker ones. This is one of the major arguments against sector-based ETFs, in which the basket of stocks is going to include a range of both strong and weak sector stocks. You can also overdiversify by holding shares of too many diverse stocks; depending on market conditions and risk tolerance, it is often more effective to own a small number of carefully selected stocks and focus attention on the trading patterns and trends of those few instead of trying to play a larger segment of the market.

3. *Mastery over the advantage (and trap) of leverage.* The concept of leverage is widely known. It is using a sum of money to borrow additional money to invest. It is far riskier than just investing on a cash basis, but leverage also has its place. Most people who buy a house use leverage when they borrow money through their mortgage, for example. For investors, it is practically automatic to be granted a margin line of credit by your broker. You can borrow up to half of the money you need to buy shares of stock. This gives you a great advantage as long as the stock's value increases.

    On the other side of the issue are the cost and risk. When you borrow through your margin account, your broker charges you interest. And if the value of your holdings declines, you still have to pay back what you borrowed. If the value of your portfolio falls below the initial margin, the difference has to be made up; that means you need to invest more cash. This is common knowledge among traders, but it helps to insert this reminder in the context of trading *risk* and reward. When you get a margin call, you should always ask this question: Is it worthwhile to keep the position open, or should my losses be cut here and now? If you want to cut your losses, you have to close the position as soon as possible. If you want to keep it open, you need to deposit funds immediately. If you do not close the position or deposit the additional sum to meet margin requirements, your broker will sell some of your holdings.[3]

4. *Control over and planning for liquidity.* One of the least-understood concepts in the market is *liquidity*. The word has several meanings, but for traders it simply means having enough cash on hand to make trades when you want to. If your capital is fully committed, you cannot take advantage of new opportunities when they arise. One of the greatest mistakes traders make is taking profits when they are available but keeping loss-position securities in their accounts. This attrition results in a portfolio fully invested in stocks that have declined in value. The illiquidity of this situation ties you up and prevents you from making any further investments even when great opportunities come along.

    A solution is to manage liquidity with a few commonsense rules. First, always keep some cash on hand. (Opinions vary, but between 5 and 10 percent of your portfolio kept in cash is a reasonable level.) Second, if you take profits, offset a portion of the gain by also selling loss position stocks.

5. *Acceptance of the constant need to acquire more knowledge.* Even the most experienced trader faces an ever-changing body of knowledge about the markets and needs to keep informed of what is going on. This is true in the overall markets and communications technology, which enables

efficient access to market information; it is also true of individual companies and their technical and fundamental information. Status of every company (in terms of price strength or weakness, emerging trends, and changes in comparison to competing from companies) is also changing every day. So knowledge has to be maintained on several levels, the basic skills every trader needs, to the company-specific attributes affecting prices and current or future trends.

Your ability to renew and maintain your knowledge base defines how much control you have over your trading experience. The more you monitor an individual company's trends and volatility levels, the better your timing becomes. With candlestick charts, you have powerful visual tools for recognizing subtle but important changes in the current trend and the beginnings of reversals and continuation patterns.

> ✓ **Key Point**
> *By knowing the popular myths of the market, you are better able to avoid the mistakes associated with them. Wise investing is often simply a matter of knowing the difference between fact and myth.*

Beyond the logical skill set you need to master technical analysis and charting, you also need to be aware of the popular myths and pitfalls that permeate the market and the trading psychology of a highly superstitious trading culture. Technicians can easily fall into one or more of these pitfalls, including

- *The tendency to think there is a secret formula out there somewhere.* Realistically, you know there is no such thing; otherwise, getting rich within a few trading sessions would be easy. The uncertainty of trading is what makes it so challenging and interesting. You cannot know the future any more than you can change the past; that's the reality.

- *An unconscious belief that an entry price is the* **start** *of every trend and that prices will always move in the desired direction from that point onward.* So many traders, even those who have been in the business for years, mistakenly fall into the trap of thinking that when they enter a position, prices will begin to move as they desire. This is based on the use of entry signals or simply on monitoring price and picking the "right moment" to jump in. But an entry price is not the zero point in a trend; it is part of a continuing change in price, affected by numerous interactions within the market. Although everyone knows this logically, not everyone always knows it emotionally, and that's where the pitfall lies.

- *The assumption that price movement is, somehow, a "conscious" element of the market.* It is easy to treat price and its trend as a conscious element, and many traders fall into this belief. It is a form of magical thinking, the belief (or desire) that something can be made to occur by the power of the mind or through outside forces (like wearing a "lucky shirt" when you enter trades). Many will not admit it, but some form of magical thinking is used widely. (For example, a trader named Dell might believe that Dell Computer stock value will rise because they share the same name.)

Candlesticks: General Observations Concerning Their Use

Using candlestick charts as a primary tracking and timing tool requires that you also have a mastery of a few basic technical theories. A short list of technical indicators is useful in determining the significance of a trend or a sudden change in price (level and direction). By itself, the chart—candlestick or other type—has limited value. Besides recognizing a specific shape to a short-term movement based on the visual development of a day's trade as seen in the candlestick, you also need to be aware of the overall pattern in the price trend. Concepts like support and resistance and patterns like breakouts, gaps, head and shoulders, double or triple bottoms (or tops), and moving averages reveal meaningful changes or confirmations in the current trend. So besides tracking the pattern of single candlesticks or a series of candlestick developments, you also need to follow the larger technical picture. The candlestick chart is the easel, and the broader indicators are the paint.

The last chapter in this book, Chapter 10, analyzes the most popular and important technical indicators. These are the essential tools for measuring the strength of trends and even the safety in the current price level of stock. So the candlestick chart provides a single source for starting the analytical task, and much more, including

- The significance of single candle signs within the context of the current trend

- Developing double moves and triple patterns of candlesticks and understanding what they mean within the larger trend

- Coordination of the candlestick formation and short-term trend with the longer-term trend revealed by the technical pattern, trading range, and moving averages

- Important signals involving a combination of the candlestick patterns, volume of trading, and technical indicators, used collectively to develop a *singular* opinion about the timing of entry or exit decisions

The simple signs and moves revealed by candlestick charts are only the starting point. Even the more complex candlestick patterns that grow from this initial trend have to be used as part of a more encompassing technical program. It is essential to learn the meanings of candlestick movements, but the two-stick and three-stick indicators that evolve signal changes of great importance.

📖 Sign

A single candlestick that provides initial indications about a reversal or continuation in the overall trend.

📖 Move

A double-stick formation that foreshadows either a reversal or continuation in the current price trend.

📖 Pattern

A candlestick formation of three or more trading periods that strongly indicates a reversal or continuation of the current trend.

✓ Key Point

The concept of confirmation *is a cornerstone of every technical system. No one piece of information should be relied upon for timing entry and exit. Every indicator is at its highest value when it is confirmed by a separate but equally important one.*

Using candlesticks as an initial indicator of what is about to occur is a wise idea because the daily price action is the starting point for the more developed technical signal. Candlesticks are early indicators of changes not only in direction, but also in emerging strength or weakness in the current trend. So if you think of the candlestick pattern in this way, the more traditional technical signals confirm the indicators first seen in the daily candlestick. The concept of confirmation is a basic idea used by technical analysts to strengthen their opinions about how to interpret price patterns.

📖 Confirmation

The use of an indicator to verify the meaning of a separate indicator occurring at the same time or earlier, consisting of movement in an index or individual stock price, changes in price trend direction, or initiation of an entry or exist signal.

No approach to price analysis should take place in isolation. This means that you cannot make reliable entry and exist decisions based only on short-term price movement seen on the candlestick chart. You also need a range of indicators stretching over the longer term, an understanding of each stock's volatility level, and the strength or weakness of the current trend. This is why you need to combine candlestick charts with other technical indicators. The more indicators you add together, the better your information pool.

A word of caution: Using too many indicators clouds the results. You need to be able to make an informed decision and confirm that decision through secondary indicators. There comes a point when you have enough data to make an informed decision, and going beyond this will not add to your information. The time element, plus the simple excess of information, then turns and confuses the picture rather than clarifying it.

Expanding the Information Pool Effectively

Beyond the technical side, it also makes sense to pay attention to a company's fundamentals, those financial values that define a company's capital strength and profitability. Even though short-term traders tend to shun the backward-oriented financial indicators, they can be used to narrow down the range of stocks you want to trade, based on price volatility and financial strength. Considering that there are thousands of stocks to choose from, which ones do you want to use for short-term swing trading and timing of entry and exit? You need some criteria for narrowing down the range of stocks you want to use. This is where the fundamentals can be valuable.

For example, you might decide to limit your trades to companies with a few important financial attributes. These could be any of dozens of indicators, but some very important ones include

1. *Basic profitability.* Even the most speculative trades can be limited to those companies that have reported growing revenues *and* profits. For some traders, the question is, Why buy shares in a company that has never shown a profit? As a rudimentary selection question, this eliminates those

troubled companies that have fallen from previous years of competitive strength as well as those that have not yet proven that they can carve out a competitive place for themselves.

2. *Strong working capital.* The ability of a company to finance its operations and pay for expansion is an essential test, perhaps even more important than profitability. A favorite ratio is the comparison between current assets (those convertible to cash within 12 months) and current liabilities (debts payable within 12 months). This is an important test, but an equally valuable one is the debt ratio. This is the percentage of total capitalization represented by debt. Total capitalization is the sum of long-term debt and shareholder's equity. If debt is growing each year, it erodes the company's ability to fund future growth. Dividends have to fall as interest obligations rise. For example, by 2008 before General Motors filed bankruptcy, its debt ratio was *over* 100 percent. This meant that the shareholders' equity was worth less than zero, which is not a good sign. A company's chances of ever recovering from such an extreme situation are very poor.

Total Capitalization

The sum of capital that funds a company's operations, consisting of equity (shareholders' capital) debt (long-term loans and bonds).

3. *Higher than average dividend yield.* Another important fundamental test is dividend yield. A company that is able to pay better than average dividends is the exception, and this itself is a sign of financial success. A company must have cash from profits to be able to pay dividends. An expanded qualification is to limit the selection to "dividend achievers," those companies whose dividend rate has grown every year for the past ten years or more.

4. *Acceptable price/earnings ratio range.* The comparison of price per share to earnings per share, or the P/E ratio, is one of the most important indicators of whether or not the price is a bargain. The P/E multiple (price divided by earnings and reported as a single number) is significant; it is the number of years' annual earnings represented in the price per share. So a P/E of 10 is the equivalent of a price worth ten years' net earnings for the company. The higher the P/E moves, the more expensive the stock becomes. As a general rule, most traders and investors like to see the P/E between 10 and 20. But as it gets higher, the risk level increases as well.

Fundamental indicators, just like technical indicators, are "rules of thumb" for a company's value and strength. Because of this, no indicators should be viewed alone. They gain significance only when analyzed comparatively on two levels. First, they have to be compared between companies in the same market sector. (Thus, a drug company with a dividend yield of 6 percent and P/E of 12 is stronger than a competitor with a 2 percent dividend yield and a P/E of 45.) Second, they have to be viewed as part of a fundamental trend. (For example, a company with a debt ratio that is falling by 5 percent per year and is now at 35 percent is more promising than one whose debt ratio keeps going up and is greater than 50 percent of total capitalization.)

> ✓ **Key Point**
>
> *Everyone needs to place a limit on the number of indicators he will watch. The most sensible approach is to combine a limited number of technical and fundamental trends.*

It's all relative, in other words.

That is the key to every form of analysis, and the same applies to candlestick charts. If you look at the charts of two competing companies, you gain insight to price strength and the current trend of each. If you review the chart along with moving averages over the past year in addition to over the past month, you advance your knowledge about that company's longer-term direction. The more expanded the field of vision, the better your information.

Chapter 2, "Single-Stick Signs," introduces the basic signs you find in single candlesticks and explains what they mean. The central lesson to remember is that, even with some exotic names to patterns and lines, candlesticks are easy to read. You can tell at a glance whether the current price movement of the stock is upward or downward, and whether it is strong or weak. Chapter 2 shows how this works.

Endnotes

1. To compute your after-tax and after-inflation breakeven, divide the current rate of inflation by your after-tax income or the difference between 100 percent and your effective tax rate (be sure to include both federal and state taxes in this calculation. The formula: *(rate of inflation ÷ (100 − effective tax rate))*. For example, if you pay a combined federal and state tax rate of 42 percent and the current rate of inflation is 3 percent, your breakeven requirement is *(3% ÷ (100 − 42))* = 5.2%. This is the rate you must earn just to cover your risks based on taxes and inflation.

2. ETFs are Exchange Traded Funds, mutual funds that have a pre-identified "basket" of stocks and trade on exchanges like stocks, rather than directly with the fund's management. Because the portfolio is identified in advance and does not change, management fees are lower because no management is required other than maintenance of the existing portfolio. However, the ETF is going to perform only at the average of all the stocks in its portfolio, including those performing well above and well below the average. For many traders, ETFs are a form of overdiversification. For others, they are an effective way to spread risk and reduce single-stock risks.

3. The rules governing initial margin fall under the Federal Reserve Board's Regulation T. This provides that you can borrow up to 50 percent of the value of securities in your account.

chapter 2

Single-Stick Signs

The most practical way to master candlestick charting is to start with the single-stick sign and evaluate it, and then move to double-stick moves, and finally, move on to the more complex multistick patterns. Each formation you find in charts is important in what it reveals about the current trend: strength or weakness, direction, or pending reversal.

Every analyst faces the challenge of interpretation. Even with an excellent understanding of how formations develop, the immediate pattern can represent a false start. Every trend has these patterns. The apparent direction or change in status misleads you if you do not fully understand how to combine many different candlestick and technical indicators, or a change occurs with no warning. Can you see patterns emerging or use candlestick analysis to anticipate the next step in a trend? That is the big question.

Uptrends and Downtrends

In all forms of chart analysis, you rely on chart patterns to determine whether the current trend is bullish (upward) or bearish (downward). This trend is not identical to the longer-term primary trend in the market as a whole. For swing traders, the "trend" is the price direction that is set for three days or more.

✓ Key Point

A technical trend is established when three or more periods move in the same direction, both on the top and bottom of the price range.

The "day" is used as a typical trading period because most people analyze stock prices from each day's opening and closing levels. Traders come in many varieties, however, so the trading period you end up using could be shorter. People wanting fast action and a lot of in-and-out of positions use the 60-minute, 15-minute, and 5-minute charts. These day traders also tend to be risk takers, so the use of short-term charts is not appropriate for everyone. References to trading periods used in this book are normally references to single-day movement.

Chart users come in many types. Some speculate but only moderately, and risk only a small amount of cash. Others use a lot of cash and leverage, and rely on small changes applied to big dollar amounts. In either case, chart watching relies on well-defined uptrends and downtrends.

An uptrend is made up of three or more periods of rising prices, but with a distinct pattern. Each day's candlestick consists of a series of higher highs offset by higher lows. So the candlestick of the second day has to exceed the previous day's high and low to qualify as an entry in a true uptrend. For example, consider the following comparison of prices:

Day	The Uptrend Pattern	The Nonuptrend Pattern
1	high 45 low 43	high 45 low 43
2	high 47 low 44	high 47 low 42
3	high 48 low 46	high 46 low 44

In this short example, the uptrend pattern shows growth in an upward direction, both in the daily high and low prices. In the nonuptrend, even though there was upward movement, it was not a trend. The subsequent high of the third day was lower than that of the second day, and the second day's low was lower than the first day's.

📖 Uptrend

A short-term pattern of three or more periods, characterized by each period's higher high price levels and higher low price levels.

A downtrend is also carefully qualified. It consists of a series of changes lasting three periods or more, combining lower lows and lower highs. A trend is set only if it consistently produces the defined results for three periods or more, although the trend can also last many more periods; three is the generally acknowledged minimum. For example:

Day	The Downtrend Pattern	The Nondowntrend Pattern
1	high 45 low 43	high 45 low 43
2	high 43 low 42	high 43 low 44
3	high 42 low 41	high 44 low 41

Downtrend

A short-term pattern of three or more periods, characterized by each period's lower low price levels and lower high price levels.

In the true downtrend, the second and third days report lower highs and lower lows. In the nondownward variety, the overall trend is downward, but it lacks the defined qualities. The third day's high is higher than the second, and the second day's low is higher, not lower, than the first. The trend ends at the point where a subsequent signal occurs, often a narrow-range day (explained later in this chapter) or other signs found in candlestick formations.

Figure 2-1 provides an example of a 90-day chart for Travelers (TRV) showing a series of both uptrends and downtrends. Note the progression of three or more candlesticks in the same direction and the conformity (in most instances) to the "rules" establishing the trend: higher highs with higher lows for uptrends, and lower lows with lower highs for downtrends. (Not all these short-term trends fit the rule, but as a guideline, it is useful as the chart demonstrates.) The points of reversal, represented by narrow-range days and other candlestick patterns, are also highlighted.

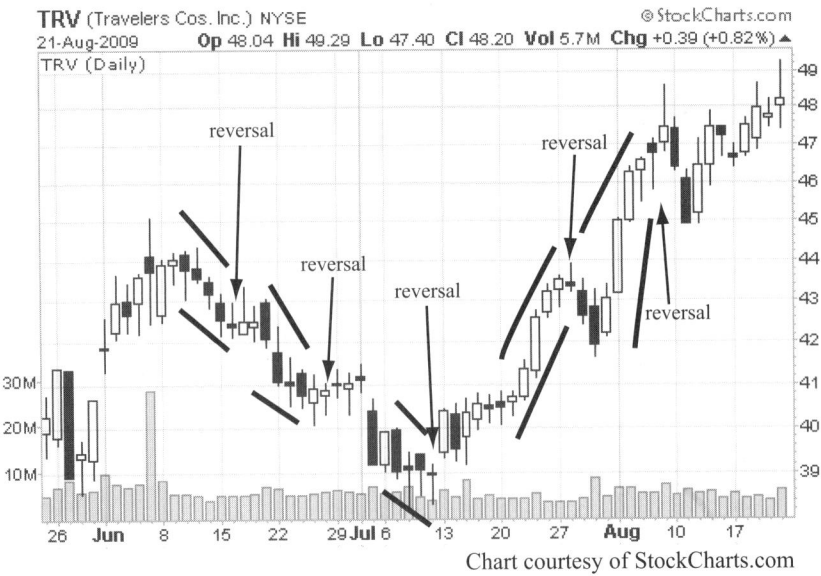

Figure 2-1 Uptrends and downtrends

The Significance of a Candlestick's Shape

As a first step in working with candlestick charts, you need to recognize what a particular candlestick formation reveals. Terminology applied to visual patterns is crucial to working with candlesticks. These terms—*real body, upper shadow,* and *lower shadow*—are important because the size of each of these components make up the signs, moves, and patterns themselves. When you need to distinguish between bull and bear patterns, or between reversal patterns and market patterns, the individual candlestick attributes take on great importance.

> ✓ **Key Point**
>
> *There is a tendency to look at the entire candlestick as a single factor in the trend, using either the real body only or the price range only. Both are important in setting trends and in anticipating reversals about to occur.*

In addition, it is important to make a distinction between the real body (the white or black rectangle) and the larger trading range. The range extends from the tip of the upper shadow (the high of the day) to the tip of the lower shadow (the low of the day). There is a tendency among technicians to pay more attention to the range from high to low, than from open to close. In fact, the OHLC chart more readily shows this range-based pattern, even though the totality of range and open-close is collectively important. The meaning of these outcomes together is important, and neither range or open-close works by itself. Candlestick terminology is somewhat different from the corresponding OHLC terminology. For example, an OHLC chart shows a "long range" from highest to lowest price, and the candlestick, with more emphasis on open-close, is described as a tall or short candle (the difference in size of the real body, which is the open-close range).

A long candle is going to take on significance as an entry in the current range, and will mean different things if the rectangle is white (uptrend) or black (downtrend). The longer the candle real body is, the stronger the move appears in the indicated direction. This trend is not necessarily revealed in the total range (as emphasized with OHLC charting) because many intraday factors might affect the range, including high volatility in the first hour of trading that is not typical of the entire day; reaction to economic news that takes place and later reverses; or higher volatile change due to rumors that are later proved to be false. So relying on range instead of open-close can be deceptive and misleading.

The long candle (also called a tall candle) can be defined as a "significant" move for the day in relative terms. Simply being longer than the previous day's candle is not significant by itself. But if today's candle is twice the extension of the typical candle range, it takes on much greater meaning. Big price movement is invariably worth paying attention to. So, for example, if a stock's daily price movement is typically in the one-half to one-point price range, an unexpected two-point candle is very significant.

The relationship between the open-close range and the shadows is also significant, another reason that candlesticks are valuable analytical tools. When a bullish long candle forms (a larger-than-average white rectangle), that is an uptrend in the day's price. However, an additional sign adds to the indication that the movement is a strong upward movement. This sign is found when the day's price opens near the low price for the full day and closes near the high. This is quickly recognizable because there will be little or no upper or lower shadow. This is an important change when the formation appears after an extended downtrend in the stock's price. It can indicate the end of the downtrend. The opposite can be interpreted when the long white candle shows up after a long uptrend. The longer-than-average price movement could signal exhaustion in buyer interest and foreshadow a leveling out and a decline in price to follow in coming sessions.

The opposite observations apply to bear long candles (black real bodies). A long black candle opening near the high and closing near the low is quickly recognized by the small or missing shadows. When this appears at the end of an uptrend, it may signal the end of the trend and a coming reversal. When this long candle shows up after a period of downtrend, it could be the sign that sellers are exhausted, which is followed by a reversal and movement in the other direction.

You may notice that longer real bodies tend to show shorter-than-average shadows. This is typical. However, what does it means when a day's outcome combines a long body with a long upper or lower shadow? As a general rule, extended shadows reveal which side (buyers or sellers) is in control. When the upper shadow is extended along with a long real body, it implies that buyers are in a stronger position; when the lower shadow is longer, sellers are calling the shots. Of course, these are generalizations and do not apply universally, but the signs and shapes are revealing when taken as part of a larger trend.

Variations on the Bullish Long Candlestick

Although the white candlestick denotes an upward movement, not all bullish days are the same. You can learn a lot from the subtle differences in bullish candlesticks to improve your timing. In some cases, a single candlestick provides you with the most important indication about the current trend or its coming exhaustion and reversal. As a general rule, you rely on a series of patterns to time buy and sell decisions; some exceptions apply when you use candlesticks.

> ✓ **Key Point**
>
> *Although candlesticks tell the most when they are part of a trend, some single sticks tell a lot, too. The long white candlestick is the most bullish of all possible formations.*

📖 Marubozu

A long candlestick, with varying lengths of upper and lower shadows. The word in Japanese means "with little hair."

The long white candlestick is the most bullish kind possible. The combined long body and small upper and lower shadows tell you the bulls were in control through the session. A few subtle variations of the bullish long candlestick are found in the *marubozu*. This is a long candlestick with varying amounts of shadow (also called the "wick" or "tail") above, below, or on both sides. In

Japanese, the word *marubozu* means "bald" or "with little hair." There are four variations:

1. *Marubozu with small upper* and *lower shadows.*

    When a long white candle appears with some upper and lower shadow and the price does not rise above the upper shadow of that long candle, two assumptions can be applied. First, the long white candle is clearly bullish and probably signals a coming uptrend in price. Second, as long as the price in subsequent days remains above the lowest point of the lower shadow, it represents a *support* level. Support is the lowest price the stock is expected to trade. (In comparison, *resistance* is the highest price likely to be traded, and the space between support and resistance is the current trading range.)

2. *Marubozu with no upper or lower shadows.*

    When there is no shadow on either end of this candle, it is the most bullish of all. This tells you the day's price opened exactly at the bottom and closed exactly at the top, with no additional range in between. When you see this, it indicates that a strong uptrend has started. Candlestick analysts are likely to use this strong indicator (along with the trend pattern and other technical indicators) as confirmation of the entry signal.

3. *Marubozu with upper shadow only.*

    Also called an opening bullish *marubozu*, this one has an upper shadow. Referring back to the first type with shadows on both sides, you can use the upper shadow to check subsequent trading; when prices of the next few days remain at or below the shadow's highest point, it is one of the two bullish signs. The second is the bottom of the candle, which has no shadow but still serves as the support level. As long as price does not fall below this level for the next few days, all signs point to an uptrend.

4. *Marubozu with lower shadow only.*

    The last type is called a closing bullish *marubozu*. The same rules for resistance and support apply, although in this instance (because the price did fall below the opening price) the potential support level is lowered for the following sessions.

Figure 2-2 shows a 90-day chart for Coca-Cola (KO), in which three of the four marubozu signs are found. The first is sign four, with a lower shadow only. The second and third are both sign one, the long body with small upper and lower shadows. And the fourth is sign three, with only an upper shadow. The less frequent type two (no upper or lower shadow) is not found on this chart.

Figure 2-2 Marubozu signs

Note that the consistency of the marubozu is not a guarantee. In this example, not every occurrence of the candlestick is followed by a strong uptrend. In fact, the confirmation is all-important. In the first number one sign (the second marubozu on the chart), the indicated bullish movement is followed immediately with a day opening high and moving downward. This occurs again in three more trading periods, setting up a downtrend and moving below the support level initially indicated by the marubozu. This was a good example of a false signal.

The Mistake Pattern

A second important formation is called the *doji*. The word in Japanese means "mistake." It is a candlestick for days that open and close at the same price level, so that there is no body, just a horizontal line. A *doji* often appears at the point where the trend is about to turn in the opposite direction. It is also the extreme version of a "narrow-range day" or (NRD), used in swing trading as a strong signal that price is about to turn and move in the reverse direction.

📖 Doji

A candlestick sign developed when the day's opening and closing prices are identical or very close; the real body is a horizontal line rather than a box.

> ### ✓ Key Point
>
> *The doji is the most extreme narrow-range day because opening and closing prices are identical or close to identical. When a lower shadow is prominent (making it a dragonfly doji), it is an exceptionally strong bullish signal.*

One of the most important bullish candlesticks is the dragonfly doji. This is a pattern in which opening and closing price are identical, but a lower shadow also forms. In other words, price fell below the open but closed at the same price as the open in spite of the day's decline below that level. In this formation, the bears dominate through the early part of the day, but before the close, the bulls take over and return price to its initial level. So the longer the lower shadow of the dragonfly doji, the stronger the bullish indicator.

📖 Dragonfly Doji

A type of *doji* with a lower shadow; the longer the shadow, the greater the bullish indication.

The lower extension of the shadow forms a short-term support level that can be used to check coming trading sessions and to identify and time your entry. But this assumed support level can also act as a cautionary signal that the dragonfly doji represents a false bullish indicator. If the following trading levels trend below the extension of the doji's lower shadow, it means the support is not holding, and that prices are likely to fall lower.

You will not always find the dragonfly doji in a perfectly flat narrow-range day. It is more likely to find one that is close, with a small trading range and even a very small upper shadow. This is demonstrated in Figure 2-3 where the quarterly chart for Exxon-Mobil (XOM) reported a dragonfly doji followed by a very strong uptrend. Note that the established support level remained in effect, showing this to be a true example of the dragonfly.

Figure 2-3 Dragonfly doji

The dragonfly can just as easily fail, establishing a false indicator. In Figure 2-4, the quarterly chart for JCPenney (JCP) shows how this occurs. A dragonfly appeared, but the following days' trading immediately fell below the implied support level.

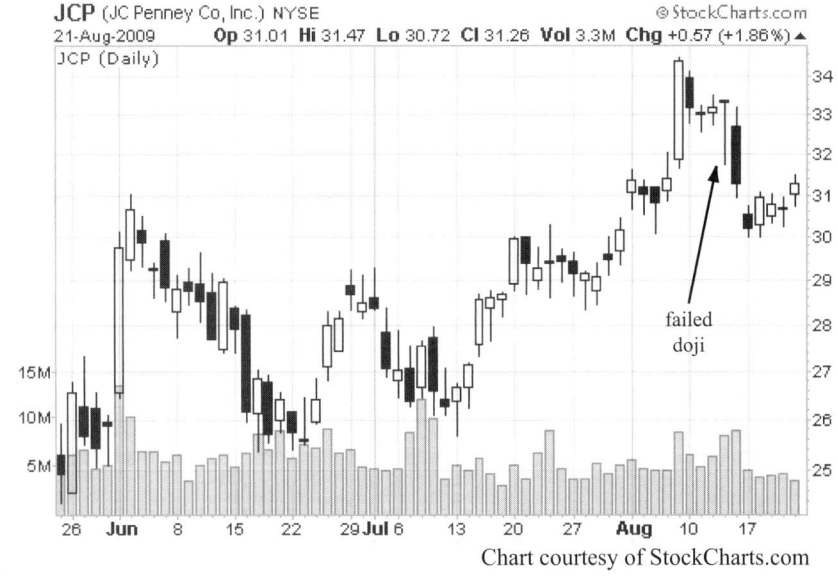

Figure 2-4 Dragonfly doji failure

This example may also be viewed as not a failed dragonfly doji, but its opposite, the gravestone doji. Just as the dragonfly is a bull signal, when the real body appears at the bottom of the stick, it is a bear signal. The ideal gravestone shows up at the very top of a bull trend; in this example, the preceding series of sessions does not conform to this criterion, but the doji still works as either a failed dragonfly or a gravestone.

Gravestone Doji

A type of doji with an upper shadow; the longer the shadow, the greater the bearish indication.

There are more kinds of doji signs, each worth analysis as part of your candlestick charting program. The opening and closing prices are identical or very close in order for the doji to form; they do not have to be exactly identical, so a doji is any candlestick with even a thin line, representing little or no gap between opening and closing prices.

Long-Legged Doji

A doji sign with exceptionally large upper and lower shadows, indicating a coming reversal in the current trend.

The long-legged doji has unusually long upper and lower shadows. This often appears at the end of a current trend and signals the beginning of a reversal. (Reversals are examined in greater detail in Chapter 5, "Reversal Pattern Analysis.") The long-legged doji is interesting because, although the period's opening and closing prices are the same (or very close), the trading range moved far above and below that level during the session. In the dragonfly, the bears took prices down but the bulls prevailed. In the long-legged variety, both bulls and bears had their turn. The bears took the price down and the bulls brought it back up, and the bulls ran the price higher and then the bears brought it back down. This action can occur in either sequence and even go back and forth many times during a single trading day.

The long-legged doji is also a symptom of an exceptionally volatile day, with a lot of back and forth in the price and, during the session, without any clear domination by either side. This is a bullish pattern when previous trading has been on a downtrend. The day's struggle between bulls and bears could be a sign that an uptrend is going to ensue. This applies especially when the pattern has established a downtrend of three sessions or more. (Of course, the opposite applies equally after three uptrend sessions and may signal the start of a downtrend.)

The signal is qualified, of course, as all signals are. Any signal is only as good as the degree to which it confirms other signs. This is as true of the long-legged doji as for any other formation. The long-legged doji signals a change in trend when subsequent price action remains above support (after the existing downtrend) or below resistance (after the existing uptrend). However, when a long-legged doji is followed by price falling below support (or above resistance), it is probably a false reverse signal. A false signal is followed by a continuation of the existing trend.

> ✓ **Key Point**
>
> *Confirmation of the doji exists when following prices remain about resistance or below support, depending on the direction. When this does not occur, the doji has to be viewed as a false signal.*

Figure 2-5 gives an interesting example of how difficult single candlesticks can be to read. This 90-day Wal-Mart (WMT) chart contains three long-legged doji days. The first and third are true, but the second one is false. The first is a two-day long-legged doji (with the second one containing a small real body); it tells you a reversal is about to occur, and this is followed by a strong downtrend. The second day sets up a high resistance level, and the subsequent downtrend remains below that level.

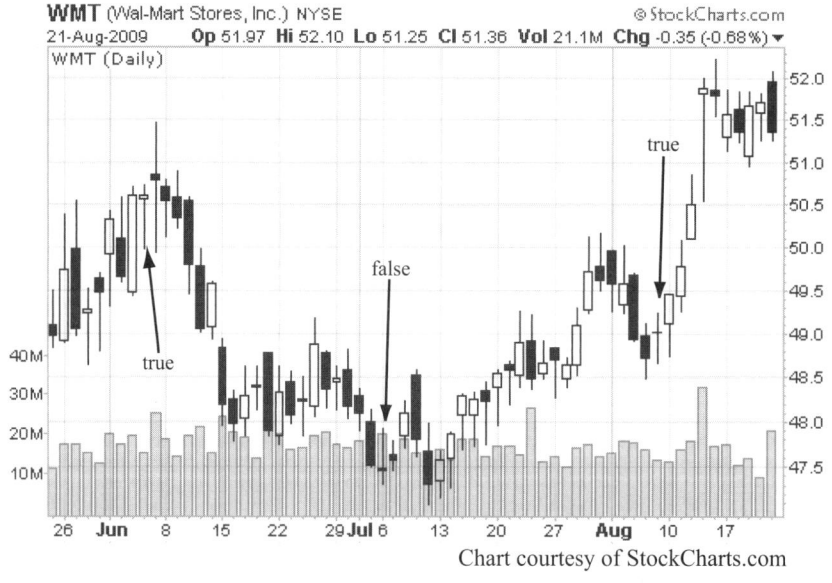

Figure 2-5 Long-legged doji

In the second of three examples, the long-legged doji is placed at the bottom of the downtrend, but the implied support level is quickly violated. Although an uptrend does follow, this particular doji does not offer a reliable reversal signal.

The third long-legged doji is the strongest of all, and it meets all of the criteria. It takes place at the bottom of a downtrend, sets up a support level, and is immediately followed by a strong uptrend with prices never falling below support.

The entry signal can also work as an exit signal. If you are watching a stock looking for the entry point, the long-legged doji (given the qualifications about false signals) can serve as a confirming entry point. By the same argument, if you are already in a position, the long-legged doji can work as a warning to close out the position. If you are long in stock and enjoying a strong uptrend, the long-legged doji could be the red flag telling you to sell. If you are short and profiting from a downtrend, the same pattern could signal you that it is time to cover the position and get out. In either case, the long-legged doji should not be ignored.

The doji comes in many additional reversal varieties. (See Chapter 5 for more examples.) As a general rule, when the horizontal line appears on the upper half of the shadow extension, it is a bullish sign (the opening price held and closed even though the bears took the price lower during the day). And if the vertical line is found in the lower half, it is usually bearish and for the same reasons; even though the bulls took price above the opening and closing line, the bears were able to bring it back down.

The Spinning Top, Hanging Man, and Hammer

Three more revealing single-stick candles are the spinning top, hanging man, and hammer. A spinning top is represented by a fairly small real body (a narrow trading range) along with both upper and lower shadows. To be a true spinning top, the candle should have two attributes present. First, the real body should be found approximately midway in the full range, and the shadows should be at least as long as the real body.

Figure 2-6 shows how the spinning top acts as a reversal signal. In the case of Google (GOOG), four spinning tops were identified, two each at the top and at the bottom of trends. These are the most effective forms of narrow-range days because they represent a trading range in which both buyers and sellers had the chance to move price, without success.

Figure 2-6 Spinning top

📖 Spinning Top

A candlestick with a relatively small real body and upper and lower shadows. The real body is approximately midway in the day's range, and both shadows are at least the same size as the real body.

The confusing attribute of the spinning top is that its color (white or black) is not the most important attribute. Rather, it is where it appears in the current trend. Swing traders look for narrow-range days (NRDs), or what candlestick analysts call either dojis or spinning tops. If the current trend is an uptrend, a black spinning top is somewhat stronger as an indicator that the trend is about to turn; and if a downtrend, a white spinning top indicates a reversal; but either a white or black spinning top can be used as an indicator of the same kind of reversal when it shows up at the end of the current trend. The difficulty is knowing when you are at the end of the trend, again pointing to the importance of confirmation.

> ✓ **Key Point**
> *The spinning top may signal reversal, but caution is wise here: This candle also forms midrange and can give out a false read.*

A failing spinning top can show up in the middle of a trend. When the color of the real body is the same as the existing trend direction, it does not always indicate that the trend is about to change direction. These signs can be misleading, so keeping a close eye on price action in the days following is necessary. As an observation of market psychology, you can even experience a series of spinning tops midway through a strong trend, none representing true reversal indicators.

Two examples of the failing spinning top can be found previously on Figure 2-3. Exxon-Mobil's chart had two of these events. The first was the single black candle midway on the uptrend at July 20, and the second was a white candle occurring at approximately August 31. These events demonstrate how important it is to (a) confirm every indicator with other signs and (b) look at what occurs on the following sessions. Exxon-Mobil (XOM) had failing spinning tops in both an uptrend and a downtrend in this chart. Both of these false signals were immediately contracted by price moving through resistance (in the uptrend) and support (in the downtrend), showing that the reversal was not taking place as the spinning top indicated.

The hanging man and the hammer look identical. A small real body is found at the top of the pattern, with a longer-than-normal lower shadow. The hanging man is a bearish signal, seen at the top of an uptrend, and a hammer is bullish, appearing at the bottom of a downtrend. To be sure that either of these is a true reversal signal, you need confirmation by trading on the following days.

📖 Hanging Man

A pattern with a small real body, no upper shadow, and a longer-than-usual lower shadow. It appears at the top of an uptrend and is a bearish day indicating an impending reversal, or it appears as confirmation during a downtrend.

An example of the hanging man is found in the quarterly chart for McDonald's (MCD). This is shown in Figure 2-7. It occurs at the end of an uptrend (which is followed by a very sharp price drop).

Figure 2-7 Hanging man

📖 Hammer

A pattern with a small real body, no upper shadow, and a longer-than-usual lower shadow. It appears at the bottom of a downtrend and is a bullish day indicating an impending reversal, or it appears as confirmation during an uptrend.

A hammer is found in the JCPenney (JCP) chart shown in Figure 2-8. There are two points, both at or near the bottom of downtrends and both acting as reversal signals.

Figure 2-8   Hammer

A confirming signal after either hanging man (indicating a true reversal of an uptrend) or hammer (signaling the reversal of a downtrend) is going to occur in the opening price of the next day's session. The indication of either signal is confirmed as a reversal only when the price begins moving in the direction indicated in the candlestick (meaning price begins moving downward after the hanging man shows up at the top of the uptrend, or price begins moving upward after the hammer shows up at the bottom of the downtrend). Like the spinning top, both hanging man and hammer can provide false signals; you need confirmation before relying on either as a reliable signal. As with most chart signs, the preliminary indication should get your attention, but you need to confirm what it appears to show before you act.

> ✓ **Key Point**
>
> *Confirmation for the hanging man and hammer occurs with price movement in the days after the candle appears. If price does not move in the direction predicted (upward for the hammer or downward for the hanging man), the signal is not confirmed; it is a false indicator.*

 The Significance of Tails

The upper shadow and lower shadow—the trading range extending beyond opening and closing prices—provide intelligence about the strength or weakness of price movement. When studied as indicators, exceptionally long shadows are also called tails.

📖 Tails

An alternate term for especially long upper and lower shadows, used as indicators of the degree of strength in bullish or bearish trends.

The longer the shadow, the more analysts tend to pay attention to it. As a general rule, a very long upper shadow is bearish because it implies that price is driven upward by buying interest that is not sustained; the ending price retreats. This indication is confirmed when two or more long upper shadow tails appear in subsequent trading sessions. A long lower shadow is the opposite. It is a bullish signal, but only if confirmed by the appearance of two or more tails over a period of trading sessions.

An example of a bearish tail is seen on the previously introduced Figure 2-7. This occurs in the day immediately after the hanging man highlighted there. This was a noticeably large tail, and on the following session, price gapped down drastically and continued in a downward direction; the total drop was about five points, or nearly 10 percent of the stock's value.

The opposite is found in the chart for Best Buy (BBY), shown in Figure 2-9. This bullish tail precedes a strong price rise. In addition, two other bullish tales appeared in preceding sessions so that a total of three out of five consecutive days showed the same indicator.

Figure 2-9   Bullish tail

The lack of demand found in a bearish tail (an "overbought" condition), meaning that the high side is exhausted and there are no more buyers entering positions, may be a sign of buyers taking profits, notably the case when price retreats following the sale of many shares. Bullish lower tails indicate that demand is growing and that the low level of prices (beneath the real body) is not going to hold, subject to confirmation.

> ✓ **Key Point**
>
> *A tail, an exceptionally long shadow, indicated the inability of buyers to sustain a growing price level (upper tail) or for sellers to hold price down (lower tail). If confirmed, the tail serves as a reliable indicator of a reversal.*

Either formation—bullish or bearish tails—can also be false. Tails appear during strong trends in either direction as part of the higher-than-average volatility in a strong trend. For this reason, the tail itself should never be used as the only timing mechanism for either entry or exit. It serves as one of many useful patterns that needs to be considered as part of a larger picture.

Tails also may indicate something different from the signal for entry and exit. They may show you where resistance or support levels are starting to be newly established. In many of the multiple-candle moves (Chapter 3, "Double-Stick Moves") and patterns (Chapter 4, "Complex Stick Patterns"), the confirming factor of an indicator is often found in whether subsequent days' prices remain lower than resistance or higher than support. Do you treat the tail extensions as these levels, or only the range between opening and closing price?

Analysts normally look at the full range of trading to define the trading range, including extensions above and below the real body. Traders tend to time purchase entry at or close to support level, and exit at or close to resistance. In other words, assuming the trading range holds, this approach assumes that price is going to continue moving back and forth between these levels, as it so often does. (The opposite moves apply to short selling, with resistance serving as the entry point and support the exit, or closing purchase transaction.) The extension of the tail on either the top (at resistance) or bottom (at support) not only indicates whether this approach is wise, but also helps you to gauge the strength of either side of the trading range.

Tail size tends to increase at these levels (larger upper tails near resistance and large lower tails at support). Remember, a tail is simply a larger-than-average shadow on the candlestick. By itself, the size of the tail is not enough of an indicator to require an entry or exit, so limiting the timing of trades to those levels is improved when the specific candlestick sign is combined with the proximity of price to resistance or support.

Another time that tails appear is when, even within the middle of the trading range, the stock is overbought or oversold. This does not always occur at resistance or support; it is normally a condition following too rapid a trend in one direction. So when prices move upward strongly, the stock is overbought; and when prices move strongly downward, the stock is oversold. At such times, tails may appear even if the price is not right at resistance or support levels. The condition (overbought or oversold) is a stronger indicator of an impending reversal and is more reliable than proximity of resistance or support, for three reasons:

1. *Trading range is dynamic*. It is easy to assume that the current trading range is fixed and permanent, but it is not. The range tends to move upward or downward over time. In fact, a reliable test of volatility is the size of the range rather than actual price levels. For example, if a stock tends to trade within a four-point range, it is less volatile than a stock trading in an eight-point range. Either of these stocks can retain the same range breadth even when their prices move upward or downward. So if you rely only on price proximity, you miss many opportunities. Tails that begin appearing after strong trends are more reliable for timing of entry and exit.

2. *Prices may move considerably within the range without approaching the edges.* The chartist who waits for price to approach resistance or support is likely to be frustrated when prices move a lot over time, but without ever reaching those top and bottom edges. The range may be narrowing, for example, so that an outdated trading range is being used and the changed conditions are difficult to spot. This is where the emergence of tails is very useful. The range is not reliable over time, but the appearance of tails at the top or the bottom foreshadows reversal and serves as a better, more finely tuned signal.

3. *The appearance of tails is more of a signal than price level by itself.* The price level of a stock is chaotic in the short term, as every trader realizes. The timing of entry and exit can be guesswork more than science, and the constant search for reliable signals is made more difficult by that short-term unreliability. There are times when price action is so erratic that no obvious trend emerges, and you cannot know whether the stock is going through an uptrend or a downtrend. However, if you see the appearance of tails, you have a strong initial indicator of price movement and you also can spot the implied direction. Getting confirmation in the next two to three sessions is crucial but valuable information. In comparison to reliance on trading approaching resistance or support, the recognition of tails is a far better system. Confirmation is essential, because even with the best single-stick indicator, no isolated day's pattern tells the whole story.

Single-stick patterns reveal a lot about the continuation or reversal of a trend as well as its strength or weakness. However, confirmation is always a requirement. The next chapter expands on this theory by showing how double-stick moves work as indicators of their own, as well as in confirming what the single patterns reveal. Single sticks are very interesting but only in the context of how they serve as signals requiring additional confirmation. With the double-stick formation, two candlesticks provide a more definitive signal that—while also requiring confirmation—a specific price direction reversal is about to occur or that the current trend is likely to continue.

chapter 3

Double-Stick Moves

One of the critical lessons of candlesticks is that you need a broad view of stock prices before taking action—some form of confirmation. As the preceding chapter demonstrated, single-stick signs hold great importance, but they invariably serve as part of a larger trend. Confirmation is the key, and single sticks often prove to be false signals of reversal. The only ways to reliably analyze candlesticks are to observe multiple formations of at least two candlestick moves, confirm what appears to be occurring, and improve future timing by anticipating changes based on solid data from more than one source.

📖 Reversal Formations

Candlestick developments signaling the end of the current trend and anticipating the likelihood that price will next move in the opposite direction.

In the trading moment when price is changing rapidly, information might seem solid enough, only to be disproved on the next trading session. This is why the trend is essential. A single-stick sign is only an entry; a trend starts with the second stick in a series. This chapter explores the strategic importance of double-stick moves to show you how to interpret information as it evolves.

✓ Key Point

To accurately analyze price movement, you cannot interpret any single day's sign as definitive. You need the double-stick move to identify and confirm reversal.

A double-stick move is defined by a setup session followed by a signal session. These can work as part of a continuation or a reversal of the current trend. Even with the use of two candles instead of one, the importance of confirming the indicated significance of the move remains. Even a double stick that appears to be a sure thing can end up being a false signal, so you need to rely on patience and keen analysis.

📖 Setup
The first trading period in a multistick formation, followed by the signal trading period.

📖 Signal
The last trading period in a multistick formation, which occurs after the setup.

Two Reversal Moves: Engulfing and Harami

A revealing sign of either bullish or bearish movement is called the engulfing pattern. In this pattern, the second day's extension of opening and closing prices exceeds the previous day's full trading range on both sides, engulfing it. A bullish engulfing consists of a downward-moving setup and then an upward-moving signal day. An additional symptom is a longer wick in the setup day than in the signal day, indicating a greater trading range and price conflict between buyers and sellers (in the downward-moving setup) and a lower trading range below the second day's opening price and above its closing price (indicating stronger bull sentiment).

✓ Key Point
When price range in the signal days exceeds the range on upside and downside (engulfs), this serves as a significant reversal indicator.

📖 Engulfing Pattern

A double-stick move in which the range of the setup period's stick is surpassed by the range of the signal period, and in which the setup stick's shadows are longer than those of the signal period.

A bearish engulfing move exhibits the opposite setup and signal. The setup is an uptrend day whose shadows are longer than those of the signal day. The signal day reverses and creates a downtrend while completely engulfing the trading range of the previous day.

Figure 3-1 provides a single chart containing both bullish and bearish engulfing moves. American Express (AXP) first shows a bullish engulfing, followed by a single but strong uptrend day; and second, it shows a bearish engulfing only a few days later, followed by six downward-trending days. Neither of these is ideal, and the ensuing patterns do not strongly follow the indication because the trends are short-lived.

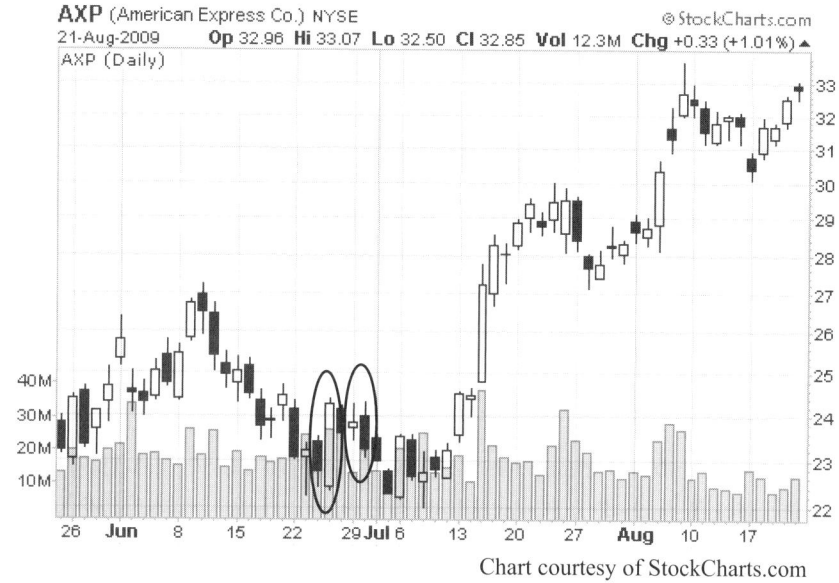

Chart courtesy of StockCharts.com

Figure 3-1 Engulfing moves

A failing engulfing move, whether bullish or bearish, occurs when price does not trend in the direction indicated or expected. The importance of confirmation apples to engulfing moves as it does to all others. In the previous example, neither of the engulfing moves was useful in anticipating the strong uptrend that followed shortly after. Failure in engulfing moves tends to occur very soon after the pattern appears, so confirmation can be found in a single subsequent trading session. Use support in bullish engulfing to confirm and use resistance in a bearish pattern. If the next day's trading range violates the established support (bullish level) or resistance (bearish level), it indicates that the engulfing move is failing.

A move opposite that of the engulfing is called *harami*. This word means "pregnant" in Japanese, so named for the protrusion in the signal day. In the *harami*, the rules are opposite those of the engulfing move. A bull harami is characterized by a downward movement in the setup and an upward movement in the signal session. The setup's shadows are longer than those of the signal, and the signal is smaller on both upper and lower sides of the range.

📖 Harami

Meaning "pregnant," a double-stick move in which the setup day's range is longer than the signal's days, extending above the high and below the low, and when the setup's shadows are longer than those of the stick in the signal period.

> ### ✓ Key Point
> *The harami is the opposite of the engulfing move; the signal day has a smaller trading range than the setup day. Even so, it also provides a strong indicator of a reversal in the current trend.*

The bear harami has an upward setup with shadows longer than the shadows of the signal. The signal session is a downtrend whose range is completely within the range of the setup. Figure 3-2 shows an example of a quarterly trading range with one bull and two bear harami formations. Walt Disney (DIS) first displays its bull harami move, followed by a strong four-point uptrend, and then shows bear harami moves at the top of two separate uptrends.

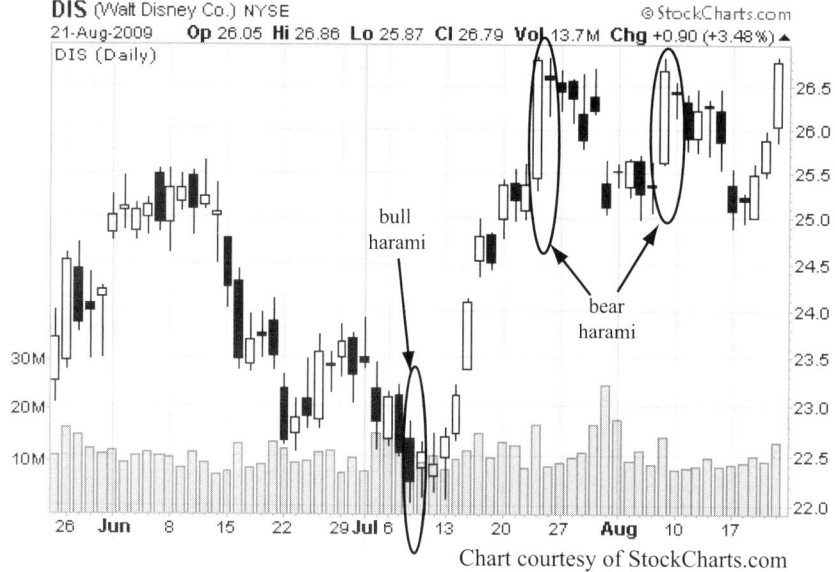

Figure 3-2 *Harami* moves

The same rules of confirmation and potential failure apply for harami as for engulfing moves. If support holds (for bull harami) or if resistance holds (for bear harami), that is a sign that the signal is real. In all four of these harami, that "rule" was observed. However, like the engulfing move, harami failure is likely to occur rapidly. So if and when you see a subsequent violation of the established support or resistance level, it indicates a failing harami. To believe in the meaning of engulfing or harami moves, you should establish immediately the direction you expect to see.

📖 Harami Cross

A type of harami in which the signal day forms a doji and is subject to the same range requirements of other harami moves.

A variation of this is the harami cross. This is a harami in which the signal day forms a doji. That is a day in which opening and closing prices are identical or very close, resulting in a horizontal line for the real body of the stick. A bull harami cross consists of a downward-moving day with the same attributes as other harami formations, and a signal day of a doji within the trading range of the setup. A bear harami cross consists of an upward-moving day followed by the doji formed within the setup's borders.

Figure 3-3 shows a chart with both bull and bear harami cross moves. General Electric (GE) exhibits a bull and then a bear harami cross. The second one (bear) forms a near-doji and the price movement that follows is what you would expect after the move, even though it did not involve a perfectly flat doji line.

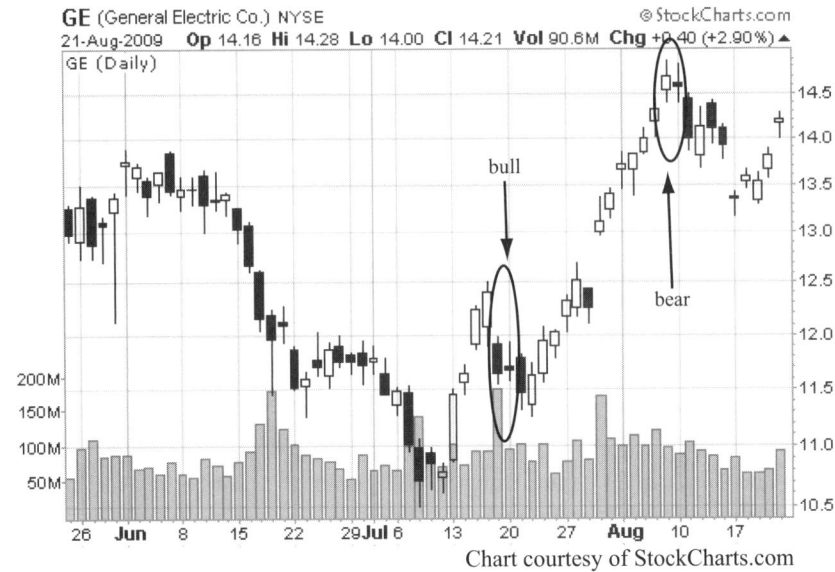

Figure 3-3 Harami cross moves

> ✓ **Key Point**
>
> *A harami cross is simply a harami when the signal day forms a doji, which is a very strong reversal indicator.*

Failure follows the same rules concerning price movement that follows. When support is not adhered to (in a bull move), the harami cross may fail; and when resistance is violated (in a bear move), the same guidelines should be observed. In the case of GE, the bear harami cross acts as you would expect; however, the bull harami cross first looks as though it is going to fail because price drops below support but then rises strongly. This problem demonstrates that any candlestick move is only an *indicator* and never the promise of certainty in coming price movement.

More Reversals: The Inverted Hammer and Doji Star

The inverted hammer is not common, but it is a very significant move when it is found, serving as a very strong indicator in the direction away from the established trend. A bull inverted hammer occurs at the end of a downtrend and consists of two parts: The setup is a downtrend long candle, and the signal (hammer) follows after a downward gap between the two periods. The hammer can be either white or black. These formations are seen in times of higher-than-average volatility.

📖 Inverted Hammer

A double-stick move made up of a downward-trending long candle, a low-side gap, and a hammer (a bull formation); or an upward-moving long candle, a high-side gap, and a hammer (a bear formation).

An example of a bull inverted hammer is seen in Figure 3-4. McDonald's had the requisite gap between real bodies, and in this instance the signal day (hammer) was followed by an uptrend as expected.

Chart courtesy of StockCharts.com

Figure 3-4 Bull inverted hammer

A bear inverted hammer consists of a long upward-moving candle as the setup, followed by an upside gap and an inverted hammer (either white or black). You would expect to see this at or near the end of a volatile period in an uptrend; it provides an exceptionally strong downtrend signal. For example, as shown in Figure 3-5, Boeing (BA) shows a large gap between setup and signal, and shortly after, the expected downtrend begins, falling 15 points in about one month.

Figure 3-5 Bear inverted hammer

✓ Key Point

The inverted hammer is one of the strongest reversal signals. The signal day follows a gap and then confirms the reversal by the hammer in which the dominant side in the current trend was not able to sustain price changes.

An inverted hammer is a valuable double-stick move, but it occurs rarely. As a consequence, it is easy to miss. The "rule" about the hammer candlestick is that it serves as a sign that price action was strong on one side of the trade; when it serves as the signal day in a double-stick pattern, it is even stronger. As with all formations, the movement in price is more significant than what any single day reveals.

The same is true for the doji star. This is similar to the inverted hammer in the formation's setup, containing the requisite long setup candle and gap. The difference is that instead of a hammer in the signal day, a doji appears. This formation is as rare as the inverted hammer and provides an equally strong indicator that the current trend is about to reverse. A bull doji star is characterized by a long downward candle, a downside gap and a doji. A bull doji star has an upward long candle in the setup and then an upside gap and a doji on the signal day.

Doji Star

A variation of the inverted hammer in which the signal day forms as a doji instead of a hammer candle.

> ✓ **Key Point**
>
> *The doji star replaces the hammer with a doji. The combined gap and price action in the signal day make this a very powerful reversal formation.*

Although the doji star is rare, both a bull and a bear version are found on the quarterly chart of United Technologies (UTX). This is shown in Figure 3-6. The first, a bear doji star, predicts a downtrend, but this does not develop for a few days; in fact, this was followed by a three-point price uptrend. This makes the point that even as a strong indicator, the doji star normally appears in exceptionally volatile times, and the UTX pattern fits this description. So the general observation that a double stick sets up support (for bull patterns) or resistance (for bear patterns) may not occur right away. One problem with this bear move is that is shows up at the bottom of a downtrend; it would be preferable to see such a signal at the top of an uptrend.

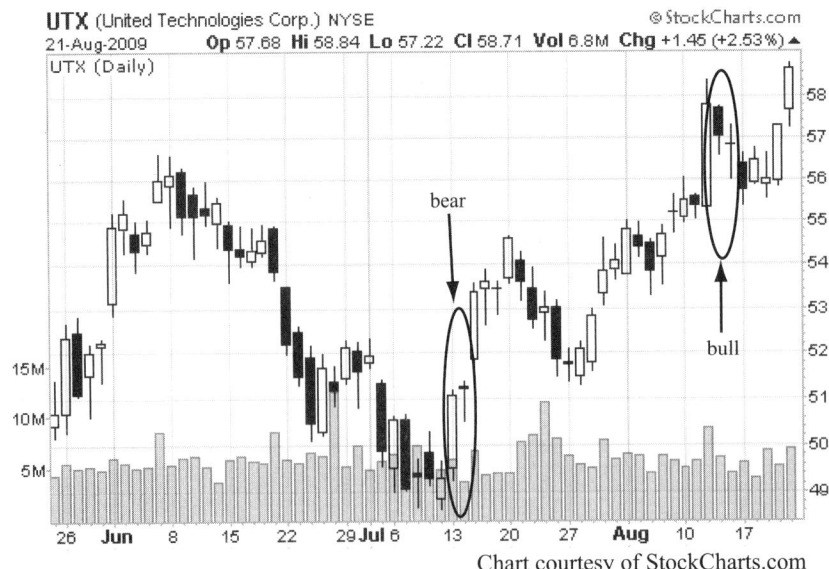

Figure 3-6   Doji star moves

The second occurrence is a bull doji star move. In this example, there is no strong trend in effect at the time, and there is a one-day delay before the uptrend takes effect. The doji star is a very strong indicator but may be followed by a counter-indicating delay. It is a volatile move showing up during volatile times.

Even More Reversals: Meeting Lines and Piercing Lines

Gaps are all-important in even a two-period trend. They usually mean that something important is taking place in the trading action between sessions. One kind of gap is invisible at first glance, and it is called the meeting lines formation. The real bodies between the setup and signal days "meet" at the same price level. On this basis, there seems to be no gap. But when the setup is a downward-moving candle and the signal is upward, there is a substantial gap—between the closing price of the first gap (bottom of the setup candle) and the opening price of the signal day (also the bottom). The gap is the span of the signal day's real candle. This is a strong bull signal.

📖 Meeting Lines

A double-stick move with the bottom of the setup day's real body meeting the top of the real body in the signal day. In a bull move, the setup day is downward moving and the signal day is upward, creating a downward gap between the closing price of the setup and the opening price of the signal. A bear meeting lines move exhibits the opposite direction in both sessions and an upside gap in between.

> ✓ *Key Point*
>
> *A lot of chart analysis focuses on the trend while overlooking the relationship of the real body between days. The meeting lines move can be very significant in foreshadowing reversal because it contains an invisible gap.*

The opposite applies in a bear meeting lines move. The setup is a white stick, meaning the closing price is at the top of the candle. The signal day is black, meaning the opening is at the top of the candle. The gap is the span of the signal session's real body. In the piercing line, the invisible gap is the difference between the close in the setup day and the open in the signal day. Depending on the comparative size of each day, the gap can be slight, or it can be quite large. A larger gap normally strengthens the indicator.

Although these moves are rare, you can find both bull and bear meeting lines in the chart for Bank of America (BAC), as shown in Figure 3-7. The gaps in both instances are relatively small, but the size of the candlesticks makes both of these valid piercing line patterns. A large gap would have made them stronger; but even with small gaps, the importance of consecutive long candlesticks acting as reversals cannot be ignored.

Figure 3-7 Meeting lines move

This is an interesting series encompassing both a bear meeting lines move and then, very quickly, a bull meeting lines move. The downtrend following the bear meeting lines lasted only four days before it ended with the bull meeting lines move. This shows that even with a strongly established change in direction, a trend can last for many days or for only a few.

A subtler move is called the *piercing line*. Like meeting line moves, piercing lines include an invisible gap. The bull piercing line includes a downward long candle in the setup and an upward long candle in the signal period that follows. The trading ranges overlap. In the bear piercing line move (also called the "dark cloud cover"), the setup is moving upward, and the signal session is moving downward. The key distinction in either the bull or bear move is that both parts consist of consecutive long candlesticks. The overlapping ranges and reversal of direction signal a change in direction.

📖 Piercing Lines

A double-stick move with two long candles. A bull formation has a downward movement in the setup and a lower, upward movement in the signal, with trading ranges overlapping to form an invisible gap.

📖 Dark Cloud Cover

Alternate name for the bear piercing lines move.

When first looking at this formation, you would expect to see it frequently. But locating two consecutive long candlesticks with reversal of direction is not a common occurrence. One chart, the Coca-Cola (KO) quarterly chart, reported a bull piercing line move and then a bear piercing line move very shortly after. This is shown in Figure 3-8.

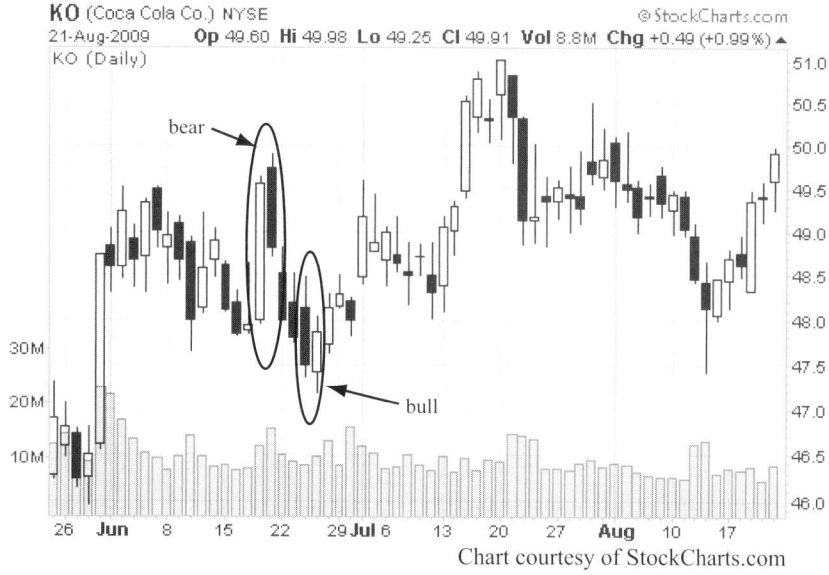

Chart courtesy of StockCharts.com

Figure 3-8 Piercing line move

✓ Key Point

Whenever you find two long candles with opposite price directions, this occurrence is invariably important and requires further study.

The initial bear trend lasts only three sessions, but the following reversal after the bull piercing lines move extends 16 sessions. The duration of any trend is where the uncertainty always lies, making timing a matter of astute interpretation of the double-stick moves like these. If you had taken action based on the initial downtrend indicated, it would have been difficult to also recognize the second reversal coming so soon after.

A recurring problem with reversal double sticks is that they often are going to be false. When prices move opposite of the direction the reversal pattern indicates, timing can be made worse instead of better. This is why you need to rely on confirmation signals and to ensure that *all* the attributes are in place. Most reversal double sticks show up at the end of the trend. So you expect to see a bull reversal move at the end of the downtrend and the bear reversal at the end of the uptrend. False signals can occur anywhere, but they are more likely to show up in the wrong place. So a bull reversal move you find within a bull trend is questionable, and the same is true of a bear reversal move within a bear trend. To serve as a true reversal formation, the move must have a trend to reverse. If you forget this important rule, you might end up buying near the top of an uptrend or selling near the bottom of a downtrend; these actions are exactly what you hope to avoid by using candlesticks, so be aware not only of the shape of the move but also where you find it.

Confirming Patterns: Thrusting, Separating, and Neck Lines

Double-stick moves are valuable when they appear as reversals (at the top of the uptrend and at the bottom of the downtrend). But how do you know when you are at the top or at the bottom? Hindsight reveals all, but in the middle of a trend, it is much more difficult to decide when it is ending. This is where double-stick confirming moves are the most revealing.

> ✓ **Key Point**
>
> *A failing move is just as important as a successful one, if only because its "negative confirmation" tells you to ignore what it seems to anticipate.*

In examining the timing of your entry and exit decisions, you should rate your ability to correctly call both reversal and confirming indicators. The failing indicators are just as important as those that succeed; the failure of even a strong double-stick move reminds you that these are only indicators and not certainties, that all the elements need to be present for the pattern to apply reliably, and that the goal is not to achieve completely perfect timing but to improve your overall success. A *confirming* indicator is different from a confirmation sign within a reversal pattern. When working with reversal, you seek confirmation of what the candlestick move seems to be revealing; when seeking a confirming move, you are looking for signs that the current trend is still in effect.

📖 Confirming Indicators

Candlestick formations that anticipate the current trend is likely to continue in the same direction.

✓ Key Point

The confirming move tells you the current trend will continue. Compared to the more popular reversal move, confirming moves can be more difficult to spot.

Confirming moves tell you that the current trend is going to continue, at least until it weakens and reverses. The duration of a trend is impossible to forecast without relying on developing patterns within the trend itself. Among these, the thrusting line is one of the most important.

A thrusting line move is very similar to the piercing line, but it confirms the current trend rather than signaling a reversal. A bull thrusting line has a long white candle in the setup and a higher-range long black candle in the signal. This creates an invisible gap to the upside (the space between the setup close and the signal open). A bear thrusting line has a downward-moving long candle in the setup and lower-range upward-moving long candle in the signal. A downward gap is created between the setup close and the signal open. Both moves confirm the direction of the current trend.

📖 Thrusting Lines

A double-stick confirming move consisting of two long candles. In a bull formation, setup is upward and a higher signal day is downward. In a bear formation, setup is downward and a lower signal day is upward moving.

The chart for Wal-Mart contains both a bull and a bear thrusting line move. This is shown in Figure 3-9. The first is a bull move anticipating continued rising prices, which is followed by an upward price movement. The second is a bear move signaling the preceding strong downtrend will continue, which it does.

Figure 3-9   Thrusting line move

The thrusting line is subtle in comparison to the more easily recognized reversal move that appears more often. Traders tend to focus on a few reversal moves, seeking exit from current strategies or entry when the direction changes; it is equally important to look for confirmation even though it is not as popular.

A second confirming pattern is the separating lines move, which looks very much like the reversal meeting lines move. In this confirming move, there are two long candlesticks and a substantial (but invisible) gap. Traders are accustomed to seeing obvious gaps represented by spaces in between trading ranges, but equally important are the differences between closing and opening prices. The separating lines move is a good example of how gaps can confirm the current price direction.

A bull separating lines move consists of a downward setup and a higher upward signal. The opening price of the setup (top of the real body) is at the same level as the opening price of the signal (bottom of the real body); the gap is the extension of the setup day. A bear separating lines move has an upward setup and a lower downward signal, with the opening of the setup the same as the opening of the signal. The gap is the length of the setup real body.

📖 Separating Lines

A confirming double-stick move creating a gap equal to the real body of the setup day. A bull formation is formed with a downward setup and a higher upward signal. A bear move is formed with an upward setup and a lower downward signal.

✓ Key Point

The separating lines move, like many other double sticks, includes an invisible gap. This should not be ignored; gaps are significant and revealing, even in confirming moves.

For example, two separating lines appear within a week in the chart of Pfizer (PFE). This is shown in Figure 3-10. The first one, a bull separating lines move, is not ideal; the sticks are not as long as you would like to see to be able to treat this as a *strong* confirming move. Even so, the uptrend does continue strongly after this appears, for the next five sessions. Then the downtrend begins, and at the same point, the bear separating lines move shows up. In a strict sense, this is not a confirming move because the trend is just beginning; even so, the price does trend downward immediately after the move shows up.

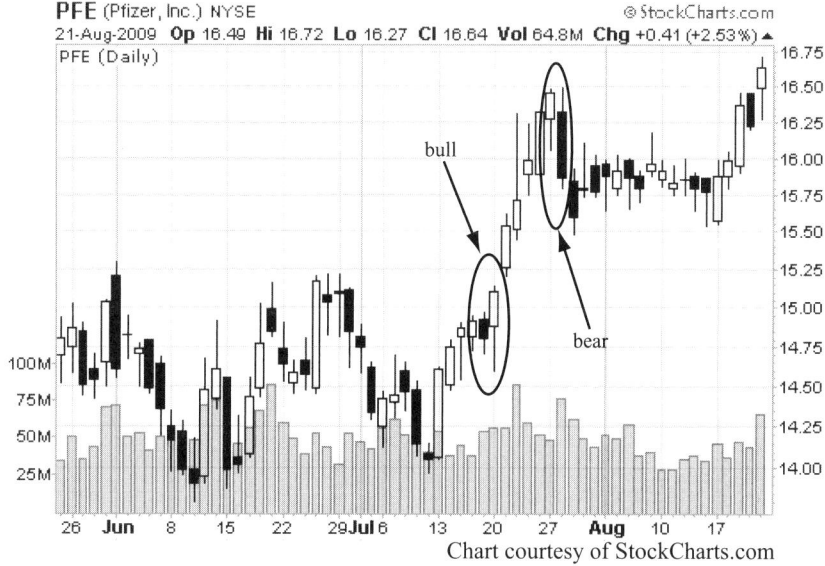

Figure 3-10 Separating lines move

These examples are not ideal, showing that a separating lines formation is a rare occurrence. If and when you do see a strong example (with long candles in both sides), the signal is strong confirmation of the existing trend.

Another version of the double-stick confirming move is the neck line, which consists of two long candles, a white setup and a higher black signal (a bull neckline) or a black setup and a lower white signal (a bear neckline). This signal confirms because the signal day opens at a gap but returns at or close to the setup close, representing a failed attempt at reversal.

Neck Line

A double-stick confirming move with long candlesticks. The setup is upward and a higher signal is downward (bull pattern), or the setup is downward and the signal is upward (bear pattern). In both cases, a gap is closed in the setup day, confirming the current trend.

There are two variations of the neck line. An *on neck* is one in which the two days' real bodies meet at about the same price, and an *in neck* has an overlap in the two real bodies.

On Neck

A variation of the neck line move in which the two days' real bodies intersect at approximately the same price level.

In Neck

A variation of the neck line move in which the two days' real bodies overlap somewhat in price levels.

The chart for Coca-Cola (KO) had three very strong bull neck lines, which are shown in Figure 3-11. All three are in neck variations of the move. It is unusual for so many similar indicators to appear in close proximity, but this could also be viewed as exceptionally strong confirmation. In fact, if these are viewed as part of a single confirming trend in a longer-term uptrend, the multiple confirming patterns are very positive signs that price levels are going to trend upward. This longer-term trend is outlined on the chart.

3 Double-Stick Moves

Chart courtesy of StockCharts.com

Figure 3-11 Neck line move (bull)

> ✓ **Key Point**
>
> *A confirming move can relate to a very short-term trend or, when multiple versions of the same move appear, may provide strong confirming signs of continuation in the longer-term trend.*

It is much more typical for confirming moves to apply to short-term trends. For example, in Figure 3-12, the Disney chart has two bear neck lines that could represent confirmation of two short-term bear trends, or as two confirmations of a single, longer-term downtrend as highlighted on the chart.

Figure 3-12 Neck line move (bear)

Reversal and Confirming Moves—Relative Values

Most chartists are comfortable with reversal moves because they represent action points. These are entry and exit signals calling for immediate action (upon confirmation, of course). So a reversal move contains a few important attributes:

1. It provides a sign that the trend is turning.
2. The action—entry or exit—is indicated in the candlestick shape.
3. Confirmation is often straightforward, represented by the next day's price action, changes in trading volume, or changing shadows *and* real bodies of the candles involved.

Reversal is considered the most important point in the trend because it signals the end of the current trend and the beginning of the next trend. If this point seems obvious, it is not. The indicator can be a false sign as well as a true one, which is why timing is only made better with the all-important confirming move and with the lack of any contradictory signs (for example, reversal moves immediately after the confirming formation).

> ✓ **Key Point**
> *Reversal moves are popular because, as timing signals, they tell you when and where to make a decision, either entry or exit.*

A confirming move tells you the right action is to *hold*, whereas reversal moves signal the time to buy or sell. The hold action is just as important as a buy or sell decision, and is an equally important attribute of timing based on chart analysis. The confirming move is the sole indicator telling you the trend has not yet ended. Even though most traders are accustomed to looking for reversal moves, confirming moves should be a part of your analysis as well. Using both reversal and confirming moves can double your effectiveness. Knowing when to act is a key to success, but knowing when not to act is just as important.

> ✓ **Key Point**
> *Confirming moves are just as important as reversals in the sense that they tell you when not to act. Instead of a buy or sell indicator, the confirming moves tell you to hold.*

To this point, focus has been on single candlestick signs and double candlestick moves. The next chapter delves into the complex pattern involving three or more candlesticks. These are more difficult to find than double-stick moves but can also act as initial *and* confirming indicators.

chapter 4

Complex Stick Patterns

Any pattern of three or more candlesticks appearing without breaks is a *complex* pattern. Three-stick patterns are stronger indicators than two-stick moves, as you might expect. Another point worth remembering is that a complex pattern is not limited to only three consecutive sticks. A pattern can easily become a trend when it moves beyond three sticks. Complex patterns can be divided into two broad categories. Reversal patterns appear at or near the end of the current trend and anticipate a change in the opposite direction. Directional patterns are indicators pointing to a new trend as it develops or as continuation of an existing trend.

📖 Complex Patterns

Candlestick formations consisting of three or more consecutive trading sessions and creating one of several specific reversal or directional indicators.

✓ Key Point

A complex pattern is simply any pattern with three or more candles.

Complex patterns are frequently extensions from established two-stick moves. These patterns can indicate reversal of an existing trend or establishment of a new trend.

The third entry into the pattern either confirms what the two-stick move indicated or contradicts it. The three-stick pattern is worth waiting for when you see a two-stick move, to confirm that the timing hinted at in the two-stick move is strong enough for you to take action.

Although complex patterns involve a series of requirements including direction of each stick, gaps, and the relationship between each session, a few observations are worth keeping in mind:

1. *The rules are guidelines, not absolute requirements.* You might discover some complex patterns with *most* but not all the requirements. For example, a third stick in a three-stick move might open slightly above the trading range of the second stick. Does this negate the indication? No, it only modifies the strength of what the formation tells you. The candlestick analysis is intended not to adhere to a strict set of rules, but to provide meaningful hints about how to improve the timing of entry and exit.

2. *No formation is a guarantee, only an indicator.* Not every formation will be followed by price movement in the direction indicated. The purpose of chart analysis is to improve your timing, but there are no assurances. Formations also fail. However, when analysis is performed consistently, complex patterns are likely to improve your overall experience and timing.

3. *Complex patterns are excellent forms of confirmation of two-stick moves.* You will notice that the majority of complex patterns are extensions of two-stick moves introduced in the preceding chapter. The complex pattern is not always distinct; it is often the case that the third entry into the formation strengthens what the first two sticks indicate and serves as a good confirmation tool for the initial pattern.

4. *The actual prediction may not occur in a strict sequence of three or more sessions.* Some chart watchers are "purists" about candlesticks, and they recognize a pattern only when there are three or more sticks that adhere in strict sequence to the required pattern. But as you study charts presented in this chapter, you are likely to observe that in some cases, a strong complex pattern will be found over a four-day period, with the second or third day a passing or nonconforming phase. Thus, the complex pattern evolves in a nonconsecutive sequence. The danger of stretching patterns over a period that includes nonconforming days is that you can easily twist the pattern to suit what you want to see or what you think should be taking place. But when an interim stick does not violate any trading range borders for the sticks on both sides and when the adjusted pattern is exceptionally strong, you can consider it as a valid complex pattern. It is a matter of judgment. Check what price action follows an "interrupted pattern" of this type to decide whether allowing exceptions within the pattern is productive or distracting.

> **✓ Key Point**
> *Flexibility in interpreting complex patterns aids in improving your timing. Specific patterns are most valuable when they adhere to their requirements, but the complex pattern can also include interim sessions not part of the formation.*

Reversal Trend Change Patterns

The first setup of complex patterns deals with reversals in an existing trend. This means that you would expect to see these formations at or near the end of an existing trend. A reminder, however: Formations do not always appear when you expect them, and they are never completely reliable. They only indicate the likelihood of changes to come.

The first among these is the three (or more) candles moving consecutively and in the same direction. An upward formation is called *three white soldiers* and consists of three white candles, each with higher high and higher low opening and closing prices. A downward formation is called *three black crows* and consists of three sessions with lower lows and lower highs in the space between opening and closing.

📖 Three White Soldiers

A complex candlestick formation consisting of three or more consecutive upward candles. Each has a higher opening and a higher closing than the previous candle.

📖 Three Black Crows

A complex candlestick formation consisting of three or more consecutive downward candles. Each has a lower opening and a lower closing than the previous candle.

Figure 4-1 contains an example of both formations on a single chart. In this example of American Express (AXP), the three black crows pattern appears first and marks the beginning of a one-month downtrend spanning about five points. The much stronger three white soldiers pattern (actually consisting of eight consecutive upward sessions) also begins a one-month trend spanning ten points.

Trading with Candlesticks

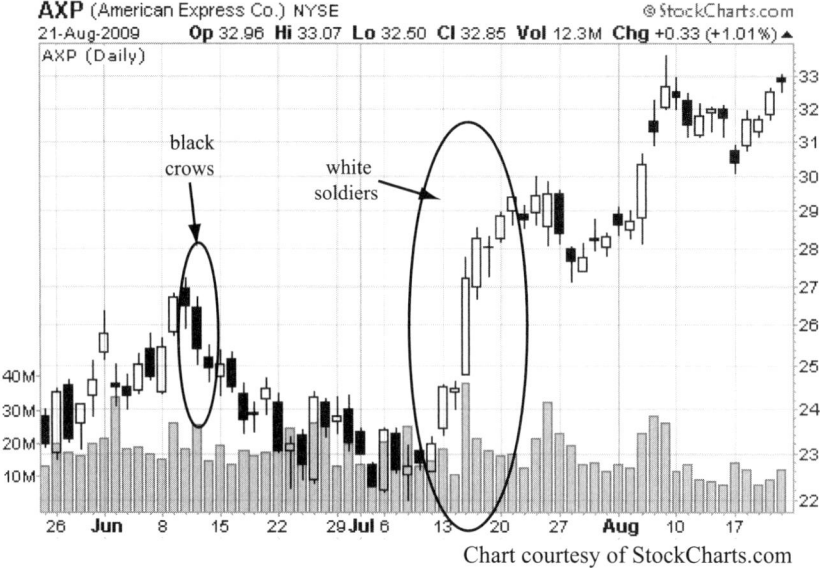

Figure 4-1 White soldiers and black crows

> ✓ **Key Point**
>
> *You are likely to spot complex patterns over a three-session period. But they can extend for a much greater number of sessions as well. The number three is only the minimum.*

Not all formations move upward or downward. A second variation of the three-stick formation is the squeeze alert. A bull squeeze alert contains three consecutive black candles, with each session's candle representing a lower high and a higher low than the previous. When this forms with three consecutive candles, with the first session a downward-moving one, it is a *bull squeeze alert*. In its strictest definition of this pattern, only the first candle needs to be black; the other two can be either upward or downward. However, the strongest possible indicator is found where the shrinking range of all three days moves in the same direction.

📖 Bull Squeeze Alert

A three-session candle with the first one downward, the second with a narrower opening and closing range, and the third with yet narrower ranges. Although the second and third session candles may be upward or downward, the strongest version of the squeeze alert contains three black candles.

An example of the bull squeeze alert with all-black candles is found in Figure 4-2. Alcoa (AA) signaled a strong uptrend with its opening bull squeeze alert in the early portion of the chart. The fact that the three-day formation was followed by a small gap to the upside was a good confirmation signal.

Figure 4-2 Bull squeeze alert

The opposite observation applies to a *bear squeeze alert*. The first candle has to be upward moving. The second and third are smaller in terms of range between high and low and can be either upward or downward, but the strongest signal is acquired when all three days are upward moving.

📖 Bear Squeeze Alert

A three-session candle with the first one upward, the second with a narrower opening and closing range, and the third with yet narrower ranges. Although second and third session candles may be upward or downward, the strongest version of the squeeze alert contains three white candles.

An example of the bear squeeze alert is shown in Figure 4-3. Cisco (CSCO) was near the end of a strong uptrend and, as always, it is difficult to identify when a current trend is coming to an end. The bear squeeze alert is an exceptionally strong indicator that the direction is about to turn. Within a few sessions, this comes to pass, although the downtrend is quite short-lived.

Chart courtesy of StockCharts.com

Figure 4-3 Bear squeeze alert

✓ Key Point

Not every complex pattern will result in an immediate reversal of the trend. A delay in reaction makes analysis more difficult.

Reversal Trend Inside and Outside Formations

A second range of complex patterns forecasting reversal is the inside and outside pattern. The first of these, the inside pattern, consists of a harami followed by a strong move in one direction or the other. The harami is a two-stick move with two attributes: the two sessions have opposite-colored real bodies, and the second day is smaller in both opening and closing price. The *inside up* (bull) move contains a black first day followed by two white days fitting this distinct pattern.

📖 Inside Up

A three-stick formation with a bull harami in the first two sessions (a black first day and a smaller white second day in a narrower range) and then a third upward day.

An example of the inside up is found in Figure 4-4. Apple (AAPL) price was gradually declining in a weak downtrend, which ended when the inside up pattern appeared. This signaled a reversal, and as expected, prices began moving upward immediately. It was the beginning of a 30-point rise over two months.

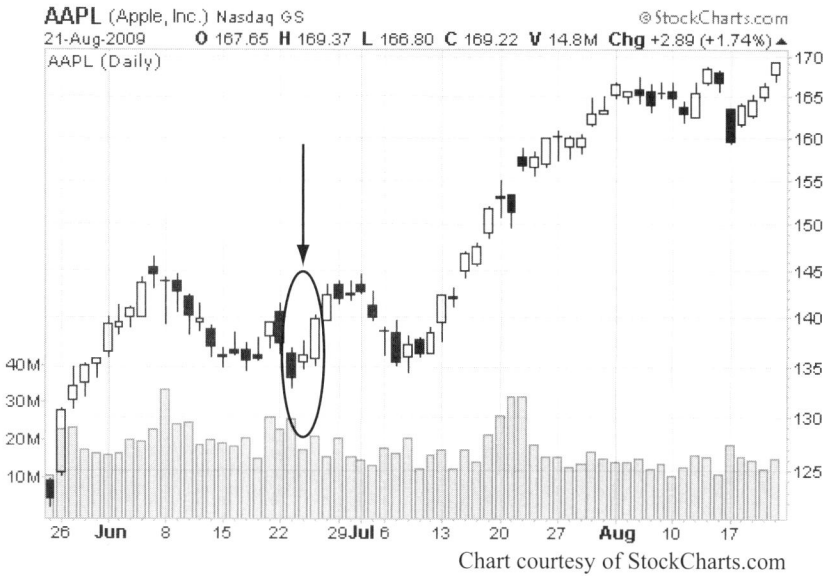

Chart courtesy of StockCharts.com

Figure 4-4　Inside up

In the *inside down* (bear) pattern, the opposite takes place. A bear harami shows up. (An upward first day is followed by a smaller downward second day, followed by a third stronger downward movement.)

📖 Inside Down

A three-stick formation with a bear harami in the first two sessions (a white first day and a smaller black second day in a narrower range) and then a third downward day.

✓ Key Point

The complex pattern is commonly a two-stick move with confirmation in the third stick. The inside down formation is a good example, strengthening what is implied in the initial harami of the first two sessions.

An example of the inside down is shown in Figure 4-5. Alcoa (AA) ended a strong uptrend, after which prices retreated back to the low level of the previous uptrend, before again reversing direction. This was a very strong signal that properly identified the timing for a trade decision.

Figure 4-5   Inside down

The second formation is the outside type. Just as the inside up or down begins with a harami, the outside begins with an engulfing move. An *outside up* begins with a bull engulfing (a downward candle followed by an upward candle with a higher high and a lower low in the opposite direction) and then a third candle moving in the same direction as the second. The outside variety is as strong as the inside.

Outside Up

A complex pattern consisting of a bull engulfing (two sticks made up of a black day and then a larger white day with higher high and higher low) and a third day moving higher.

📖 Outside Down

A complex pattern consisting of a bear engulfing (two sticks made up of a white day and then a larger black day with higher high and higher low) and a third day moving lower.

An example of one chart with both an outside up and an outside down is shown in Figure 4-6. Best Buy (BBY) presents an interesting picture of these patterns. Although normally reliable, the outside up fails, because price immediately takes a downward movement that lasts about one month. The outside down has a delayed reaction; prices continue upward for two points before the predicted downtrend kicks in. These two patterns demonstrate that no formation is completely reliable and that the indicated price movement does not always occur immediately after it appears.

Chart courtesy of StockCharts.com

Figure 4-6 Outside up and down

Reversal Stars and Abandoned Babies

Some reversal three-stick patterns are less visible than others, and like other patterns, these less visible ones combine previously explained two-stick moves with a third component. This third consecutive day's movements strengthen the indicated change in direction.

> ✓ **Key Point**
>
> *Some of the most valuable reversal indicators involving complex patterns are not obvious. The less visible pattern provides valuable confirmation and is worth looking for; most chart watchers will spot the obvious patterns easily, but it takes greater powers of observation to find the less visible ones.*

The first of these patterns is the *morning star*, a bull indicator showing up at the end of a downtrend. It consists of a bull inverted hammer (a downward day, downward gap, and upward day) followed by another, higher upward day.

📖 Morning Star
A bull three-stick pattern combining a bull inverted hammer with a subsequent third day moving upward.

The morning star, like the inverted hammer, does not always succeed. It is simply an indicator and not a promise of coming price direction. For example, in Figure 4-7, McDonald's price trend concluded a strong upward movement with a morning star. Because this came within an uptrend, it may have been viewed as a false signal (which it was) or a type of confirmation that the trend was going to continue (which it did not). The fact that this did not appear during a downtrend is a good clue that it was a false signal.

4 Complex Stick Patterns

Chart courtesy of StockCharts.com

Figure 4-7 Morning star

The *evening star* is the bear version of the same formation. It consists of a bear inverted hammer (an upward day and upward gap) followed by a downward day moving lower. The chart of Intel (INTC) anticipates a mild downward movement, which is shown in Figure 4-8. In this case, the bear indicator appears where it should be, after an uptrend.

📖 Evening Star

A bear three-stick pattern combining a bear inverted hammer with a subsequent third day moving downward.

Figure 4-8 Evening star

Neither the morning star nor the evening star in these two examples demonstrates how these patterns work as reversals. The first was a false indicator, and the second came before a mild downtrend. Even so, the evening star is worth paying attention to when it appears at the end of the trend.

A similar pattern is the abandoned baby, which is an expansion of the two-stick doji star. In the *bull abandoned baby*, the bull doji star (a downward day, downward gap, and doji) is followed by an upward gap and then an upward day. The doji, residing all by itself between two gaps, is the "abandoned" segment of this formation.

Bull Abandoned Baby

A complex pattern consisting of a bull doji star (a downward day, downward gap, and doji) followed by an upward gap and then an upward day.

An example of the bull abandoned baby is the case of Bank of America (BAC). In Figure 4-9, the downtrend concludes with a bull abandoned baby and then a strong uptrend. It is also interesting to note that the uptrend stalls and shows four downward sessions before resuming more strongly.

✓ Key Point

The abandoned baby pattern is a strong indicator because of the reversal after the doji day. This tells you the direction supported by the pattern has a lot of strength.

Figure 4-9 Bull abandoned baby

A *bear abandoned baby* is the opposite. It is the combination of a bear doji star, a gap, and a downward day. Figure 4-10 provides an example in the case of DuPont (DD). Here, the pattern shows up at the top of an uptrend, as you would expect. The abandoned portion (a very narrow trading range day representing a near-doji) fits the pattern and predicts the reversal accurately, with prices immediately moving into a downturn, moving down six points over the next month, and then creating a double bottom before rallying once again.

📖 Bear Abandoned Baby

A complex formation consisting of a bear doji star (an upward day, upward gap, and doji) followed by a downward gap and then a downward day.

Figure 4-10 Bear abandoned baby

Complex Trend Patterns

Besides easily recognized reversal patterns, some complex patterns create or confirm a trend. These trend patterns should be expected to appear either after a period of sideways trading (representing uncertainty) or in highly volatile trends where no apparent direction has been previously set. The trend patterns forecast a direction, either immediately or after a brief delay in price movement.

The first of these are the side-by-side white lines (bull) and black lines (bear) patterns. The distinction of these formations to those following is that the white line formations are bullish and the black line formations are bearish. (In comparison, the next ones involve bullish black and bearish white side-by-side formations.)

Side-by-Side White Lines Bull

A pattern of three white sessions. The first is followed by an upside gap and then two additional upward-moving sessions.

📖 Side-by-Side Black Lines Bear

A formation of three black sessions. The first is followed by a downside gap and then two additional downward-moving sessions.

An example containing several of these side-by-side patterns is shown in Figure 4-11. Verizon (VZ) has three distinct side-by-side lines, two white lines (bull), and in the middle, one series of black lines (bear). Even though prices appear to be quite volatile in this period, the side-by-side formations accurately predict short-term price direction. The gap with continued direction afterward makes this a strong indicator in either direction.

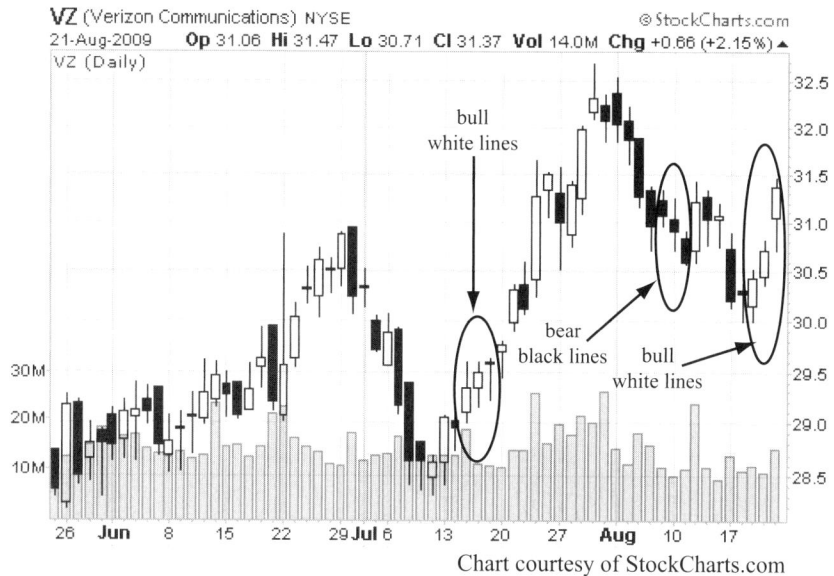

Chart courtesy of StockCharts.com

Figure 4-11 Side-by-side bull (white) and bear (black) lines

The opposite version of side-by-side lines is also going to be found. The side-by-side portion of the formation refers to the second and third days, and this is where you find the reverse of the white (bull) and the black (bear) interpretation.

A bull side-by-side black lines pattern consists of an upward session, an upward gap, and two downward sessions. In this instance, even though the second and third sessions are black, the upward gap after the first session is the important sign. This is most likely to be found during an uptrend. The pattern reveals that although trading during the second and third sessions moved in a bearish direction, the price trend did not fill the gap, creating new support at the lower extension of the first day's range and making the pattern bullish.

📖 Side-by-Side Black Lines Bull

A formation of one white session, an upside gap, and two black sessions. Price support prevents the bears from moving price down to fill the gap and forms new support, making this a bullish indicator.

For example, Figure 4-12 shows how Johnson & Johnson (JNJ) prices acted during a mild uptrend with some sideways movement. The side-by-side black lines formation preceded a strong upward movement. Note also how the lower shadow of the first day created a new line of support in trading after the side-by-side formed.

Figure 4-12 Bull side-by-side black lines

The bearish version of this, the side-by-side white lines bear formation, contains the opposite attributes and creates a new level of resistance at the top of the first day's trading range. The downward gap is followed by further downward price movement as bulls prove to be unable to fill the gap.

📖 Side-by-Side White Lines Bear

A pattern of one black session, an upside gap, and two white sessions. Price resistance prevents the bulls from moving price up to fill the gap, making this a bearish indicator.

For example, Exxon Mobil (XOM), shown in Figure 4-13, reveals a bearish side-by-side white lines pattern after the existing uptrend had already begun to weaken. The trend had stalled over the previous two weeks, and the next price direction was uncertain, at least until the bearish side-by-side showed up. Price levels then tumbled nine points over one month, which was predicted by the side-by-side. It's the gap in trading between days, followed by no reversal and fill, which signals the trend.

Figure 4-13 Bear side-by-side white lines

> ### ✓ Key Point
> *Side-by-side patterns are strong because they reveal a gap followed by the lack of reversal or fill. This is a very strong sign of support for the direction forecast.*

Complex Gap Trends

A *tasuki* is a Japanese sash used to hold up a shirt sleeve, similar to a garter. The *tasuki* gap pattern is so-called due to the shape of the three sticks. The first session is followed by a gap and then "held up" by the second and third session's price movement. An upside (bull) tasuki gap contains an upward day followed by an upside gap and then a second upside day followed by a somewhat lower range. This pattern opens within the range of the second day and finishes below it. In this pattern, usually found either within an uptrend or after a period of sideways trading, the important element is that even with the third day moving to the downside, the gap holds up; this is why the pattern is bullish. Although this portends an uptrend, the result might be delayed by several trading sessions.

Upside Tasuki Gap

A complex pattern creating a bull trend with an upward candle, an upside gap, a second upward candle, and then a downside candle that does not fill the gap. It is a bull formation because the gap holds up.

A downside tasuki gap consists of a downward candle, a downside gap, a second downward candle, and then an upside candle. The third candle opens within the trading range of the second session but does not move high enough to fill the gap. This inability to take prices back to previous trading levels defines the formation as a bear trend.

Downside Tasuki Gap

A complex pattern creating a bear trend with a downward candle, a downside gap, a second downward candle, and then an upside candle that does not fill the gap. It is a bear formation because the gap holds up.

> ✓ **Key Point**
>
> *A tasuki gap is exceptionally strong because the price direction is maintained without a fill of the gap or price reversal.*

For example, Disney (DIS) saw one of each type of tasuki gaps in its chart, as shown in Figure 4-14. First was a downside tasuki anticipating the modest decline that followed. Second was a stronger upside tasuki gap that forecast a stronger uptrend. This does not meet the strict definition of the formation because the third candle opened not within the range of the second but slightly above, but it is always the case that the shape of a formation is more significant than strict adherence to all its requirements.

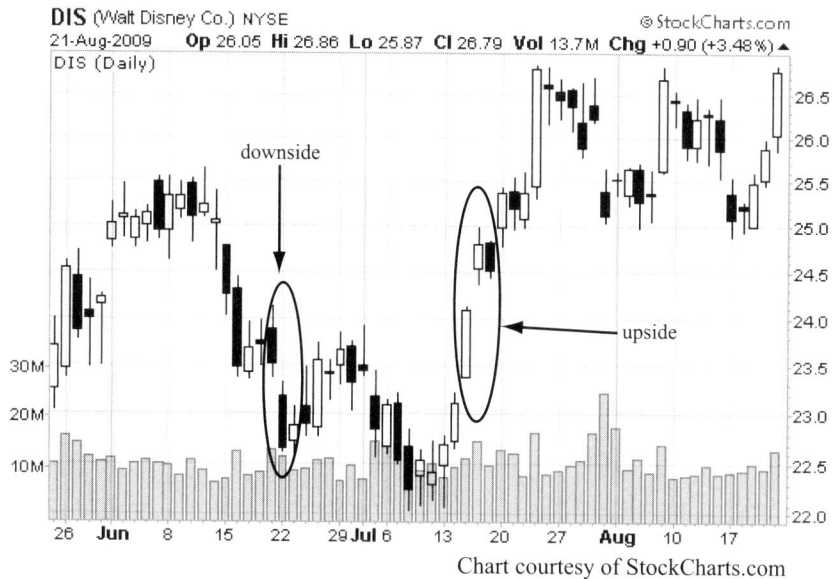

Figure 4-14 Tasuki gaps

The tasuki is a strong indicator because the gap does not get filled by subsequent price movement. If a gap is a common gap (one occurring frequently in the course of normal trading), you expect it to fill within a short time. So a nonfilled gap becomes very important in setting up or reinforcing a trend. In comparison, a filled gap is similar to the tasuki, but the gap does get filled.

The distinction is that in the filled gap, the low of the first session (in a bull pattern) is not violated. In the bull filled gap pattern, the opening price of the first session sets a support level, and this is confirmed by the third session. So an *upside gap filled* consists of an upward session, an upside gap, a second upward session, and then a downward session that fills the gap but does not fall below support.

📖 Upside Gap Filled

A bull complex pattern with an upward session, an upside gap, a second upside session, and then a third session moving to the downside. However, although the third session fills the gap, it does not fall below the support level set by the first day's opening price.

An example of an upside gap filled was found on the chart of Home Depot (HD), seen in Figure 4-15. This chart actually contains two examples in a short period of time. The first one is strong because the established support level is respected for the next few sessions. The second upside gap filled presents a problem. Although the support level was not violated within the pattern itself, the following sessions were more difficult to read. The price level fell immediately below the support level set by the second upside gap filled, and in fact even violated the support level set by the first formation. The price did move upward after this departure, but as far as timing based on this unfolding of events, the indication was confused by the subsequent price action.

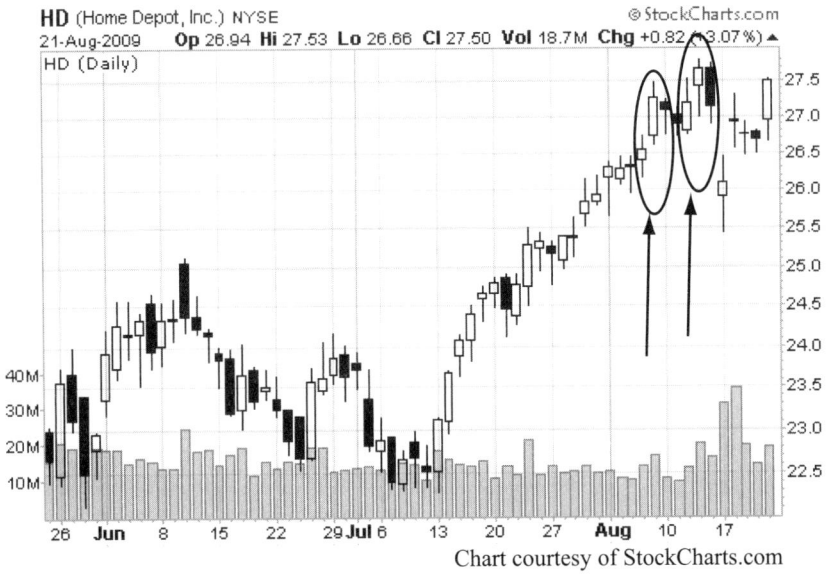

Figure 4-15   Upside gap filled

> ✓ **Key Point**
>
> *The established support (bull) or resistance (bear) levels define the success of a gap filled pattern. It often occurs that price moves strongly in the direction opposite of the gap, so when this does not take place, it reserves more attention.*

A *downside gap filled* is the opposite. It consists of a downward session, a downside gap, a second downward session, and then an upside movement that (a) fills the gap and (b) does not violate the newly set resistance level of the first session's opening price.

📖 Downside Gap Filled

A bear complex pattern with a downward session, a downside gap, a second downside session, and then a third session moving to the upside. However, although the third session fills the gap, it does not move above the resistance level set by the first day's opening price.

An example of a downside gap filled is that of Boeing (BA), seen in Figure 4-16. This chart contains two very strong downside gap filled patterns meeting all the criteria. The first occurred after price levels topped off and a brief period of sideways trading took place. The second followed a very strong and unusual unfilled downside gap. When you see a gap like this, you need to pay close attention to patterns that follow because it could indicate a reversal. In this case, the downside gap before the second downside gap filled took place after several sessions of strongly falling prices, so the question at that point had to be: Is the price trend about to reverse? The answer is found in the downside gap filled coming immediately after the big gap. The resistance level set by the three session pattern held for another five points of decline before prices did reverse and begin moving up.

Figure 4-16 Downside gap filled

Whether patterns reverse the established trend, confirm existing movement, or set a new trend, it pays to observe them as they emerge. Any unusual developments, including exceptionally long days (or short days represented in the doji day), big increases in volume, or price gaps, indicate that something is about to take place. For most traders, the focus of interest in such developments concerns reversal. Whether used for entry or exit, a reversal signal is the key to timing of your decision. The next chapter explores methods for analyzing reversal trends and maximizing their value.

chapter 5

Reversal Pattern Analysis

So much of charting is involved with reversal recognition. As the entry and exit point for the majority of technical strategies, reversal is more widely acknowledged as an important signal than continuation patterns. When you see a continuation indicator, the prescribed action is to take no action; technicians are likely to exhibit much greater interest in identifying the best times to enter and to exit. This is how profits are maximized and losses avoided.

In earlier chapters, some basic reversal patterns were explained and demonstrated in charts. However, recognizing a reversal pattern and then analyzing it are not the same process. The analysis should include judgment about whether the signal is true or false, the degree of strength or weakness in the reversal, and whether or not it confirms another indicator (or is confirmed in turn). Confirmation can include additional candlestick patterns, moving averages, and traditional technical signs. This chapter examines the relationship between the initial reversal pattern and other signals and explores the methods of analysis that are most productive for your technical trading program.

Recognizing the Bull Reversal

A bull reversal occurs at the end of a downtrend. If a downtrend is not present, there is really nothing to reverse. A mistake made by some chartists is to overlook this crucial fact. In the desire to enter a position, you may find yourself seeing an apparent reversal pattern and then deciding to enter a long position. This is a mistake.

> ✓ **Key Point**
>
> *A reversal can occur only if there is a current trend to reverse. If this is not present, then an indication of reversal is not valid.*

An oddity of the reversal pattern is that it must show up at the trend's conclusion. The identical pattern may appear during an uptrend or in the middle of a sideways price movement. This is not a bull reversal indicator, but merely an aberration in the pattern of current trades.

To illustrate how a reversal pattern can appear in the wrong place (meaning it is not a true reversal), the following illustration of two bull patterns reveals the primary point: a bull reversal has to appear after a downtrend; otherwise, it is not reliable.

The most basic bull reversal pattern is the three white soldiers. This complex pattern consists of three consecutive trading periods, all upward and with each opening *and* closing higher than the last. You expect to see this at the conclusion of the downtrend, and when that is revealed, it is one of the strongest reversal signals. But check Exxon Mobil (XOM) to recognize a false bull three white soldiers signal, as shown in Figure 5-1.

Chart courtesy of StockCharts.com

Figure 5-1 Three white soldiers—false reversal signal

The pattern would be a very strong bull reversal indicator if it appeared at the bottom of a downtrend. This shows up at the top of an uptrend, making it deceptive. There are several ways to recognize this as a false reversal:

1. *It did not occur in a downtrend.* The most obvious flaw is as far as you actually need to go in analyzing this as a false reversal. It shows up in the wrong place, meaning there is no downtrend to reverse.

2. *It was followed by a doji and two upward sessions moving downward.* The three sessions immediately after the false reversal signal are odd in the sense that they are upward-moving days, but the price trend is downward. This is not what you expect to see in an uptrend. So even if you were to interpret the three white soldiers as a confirmation of an uptrend, the following price movement contradicts this.

3. *The period preceding this formation was very volatile to the upside, but the trend was not sustainable.* Whenever you see a fast uptrend with price gaps and no interim reversals, you have to be cautious. In this example, the previous 12 sessions were either upward-moving or doji formations. This kind of strong movement cannot always be sustained, and this is a good example of the problem this kind of volatility presents. The overly fast price increase is followed by an equally strong price decline.

Another example involves an equally recognizable bull reversal pattern, the morning star. As with the three white soldiers, this reversal signal is very strong when it shows up at the bottom of a downtrend. The pattern consists of a downward-moving session, a downside gap, a second upward-moving session, and then a third, higher upward-moving session. The third session closes the gap created between the first and third sessions.

When the morning star is seen midway through an uptrend or during a period of consolidation, there is no downtrend to reverse. For example, check Figure 5-2. In the case of Caterpillar (CAT), the false signal shows up at the end of a strong uptrend, proving that it is a false signal. There is no downtrend to reverse.

Figure 5-2 Morning star—false reversal signal

✓ Key Point

The best way to recognize a false signal is that it shows up in the wrong place. Remember, there must be a trend to reverse; otherwise, a reversal signal does not mean anything.

This false signal, like the previous one, shows up after a volatile upward movement in price. Note the price gaps to the upside in three of the previous five sessions as a sign of exceptional volatility. The signal is in the wrong place and is typical of a false indicator.

Recognizing the Bear Reversal

A similar pattern analysis works for bear reversals. The bull signal called three white soldiers has a bear counterpart called three black crows. This signal consists of three or more sessions, all downward moving, with each opening and closing lower than the previous session. To be considered a true bear reversal, this signal must appear at the end of an uptrend; otherwise, there is nothing to reverse.

The false bear signal not only shows up at the wrong place in the trend, but also is likely to appear after a significant price movement in a downward direction. A true bear reversal cannot appear at this point. Look for continuing declines in the sessions immediately after three black crows, revealing that it is not a reversal at all, but a false signal. For example, Alcoa (AA) revealed *three* separate examples of false reversal three black crows, in close proximity. Figure 5-3 shows these examples.

Chart courtesy of StockCharts.com

Figure 5-3   Three black crows—false reversal signals

What does this mean? It is unusual for any pattern to repeat three times close together, but even more unusual when the trend includes false signals. Remember, three black crows is a bear reversal, so it is valid only when it appears at the conclusion of an uptrend. In these instances, the first of the three formations meets this basic requirement. However, as the price falls three points, the second and third patterns do not conform to the requirement. In fact, the end of the third of the three patterns is accompanied by some additional pattern changes signaling a reversal of the short and moderate downtrend, rather than a bear reversal. These changes are the exceptionally high volume and near-doji session (narrow range day), both signaling the stronger likelihood of a reversal and impending uptrend. In this example, the bear reversal patterns showing up in the wrong place actually were confirmed as signaling a *bull reversal*, which was then confirmed by the doji and higher-than-average volume.

This case is very instructive. The three black crows are reversal patterns but should be treated with caution. They are not continuation patterns although some traders may misinterpret the chart to believe that when the three black crows signal appears in a downtrend, the pattern is a continuation pattern. That is not the case. A particular pattern is either a reversal or continuation but is not interchanged based on the circumstances. A bear reversal pattern is valid only when it shows up after an uptrend.

> ✓ **Key Point**
>
> *Every candlestick formation forecasts either a reversal or continuation. These are not interchangeable and cannot be substituted based on the circumstances.*

Another false bear signal is found in the morning star pattern's opposite: the bear pattern called the evening star. This pattern consists of three sessions. The first is an upward-moving session, followed by an upside gap, a downward-moving day, and then a lower downward-moving day that closes the original gap. When the evening star is seen at the top of an uptrend, it signals a reversal, and you should expect to see the price begin to decline. However, when the evening star appears at the wrong place (not at the top of an uptrend), it is a false signal. For example, Johnson & Johnson (JNJ) showed a false evening star, as shown in Figure 5-4.

Chart courtesy of StockCharts.com

Figure 5-4 Evening star—false reversal signal

This false signal was not as easy to spot as previous examples. However, the evolving uptrend was accompanied by higher-than-typical volume five sessions later and a well-established uptrend, contradicting the false evening star. Most traders will not want to wait for five sessions before deciding whether to act, but there is a better indicator of this evening star as a false signal: its placement. It did not emerge after an uptrend but followed a sideways pattern. There was no uptrend to reverse.

Whether a false signal is a bull or bear indicator, a few important rules are worth remembering:

1. *The signal has to appear at the right place.* A bull reversal has to form at the bottom of a downtrend, and a bear reversal must appear at the top of an uptrend. If this essential rule is not followed, it is a false signal.

2. *Any unexpected price movement following the pattern is suspicious.* Look for confirmation in price movement to either defer entry/exit decisions or to cut losses. You expect prices to rise after a bull reversal and to fall after a bear reversal. When the opposite movement occurs instead, it probably means the signal was not what you thought.

3. *Look for confirmation such as evolving trends and unusually high volume to pick up the false signals.* Every indicator should be confirmed, either by price movement, volume, or additional pattern development. This confirmation reduces the chance of error or misreading of signals.

4. *Reversal signals cannot serve as continuation signals.* The many formations of reversal and confirmation patterns are quite distinct. An easy trap for any technician is to decide that a reversal pattern showing up in the wrong place is actually a continuation pattern; this is not so.

5. *Remember, all signals are indicators and not guarantees.* The pattern you spot on a chart is only an indication of what might occur next, but not a guarantee. The purpose of pattern analysis is to improve your accuracy in recognizing reversals, but no one will time his entry and exit decisions perfectly.

The Doji as a Reversal Signal

Chapter 2, "Single-Stick Signs," presented a brief introduction to the doji, including illustrations of dragonfly and long-legged forms. These are two of the most single-stick moves. However, the doji comes in many additional forms, which are worth further examination in the context of reversals.

> ✓ **Key Point**
> *Single-stick attributes are extremely valuable but are made much more significant when studied within a current trend and as part of a longer formation.*

Any single-stick move has to be analyzed as a part of the current trend as well as subsequent price movement. With that in mind, the doji plays a key role in many reversal signals. You will discover that the doji tends to show up in formation of the top or bottom of a current trend. Swing traders look for the narrow-range day (NRD) to signal entry and exit, and the doji is the most extreme form of this. The characteristic of the stick—opening and closing prices identical or very close to one another, resulting in little or no real body—reveals a lot about the session's trading. The upper and lower shadows display the trading range, and the longer those shadows, the greater the significance for bulls, bears, or both. When the opening and closing prices are close but not identical, the pattern is called a *near-doji*.

📖 Near-Doji

A candlestick with an exceptionally thin space between opening and closing prices; although they are not identical, the range is so small that the candle is granted the same significance as a perfect doji.

The doji is going to show up as the conclusion to many trends. When a doji forms a top, it is a bear indicator; then it is called a *northern doji*. This basic formation is a strong bear indicator, especially if the preceding trend was strong to the upside. The stronger the short-term uptrend, the most important the top doji. When a doji appears at the bottom of a downtrend, it is a *southern doji* and is a strong bull signal. The greater the preceding downtrend, the more significance the doji has. This is especially true when the doji is accompanied by greater-than-normal trading volume.

📖 Northern Doji

Any doji appearing above a previous uptrend, considered a strong bear signal.

📖 Southern Doji

Any doji appearing below a previous downtrend, considered a strong bull signal.

Although the doji is a popular and revealing signal, it is likely to appear many times in volatile trading patterns. Many doji formations prove to be false, so they should always be confirmed by additional signals, including other candlesticks, changes in volume, and evolving resistance or support.

✓ Key Point

The doji shows up frequently, especially during volatile trading patterns. Although the doji is important, it is not always an indication of a signal that the trend is about to change.

An example of a chart with northern, southern, and false doji sessions was that of General Electric (GE), as shown in Figure 5-5. This example reveals two of each appearance of the doji.

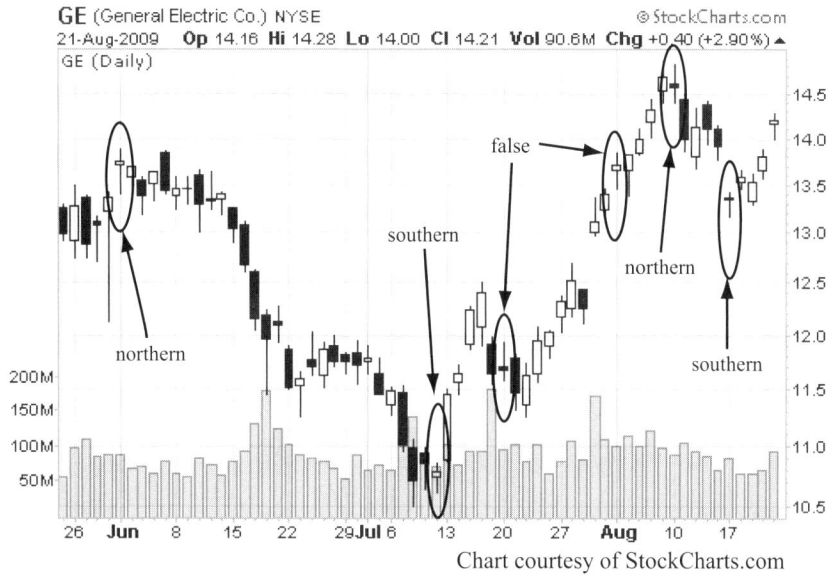

Figure 5-5 Northern and southern dojis

The false doji candlesticks in this chart are troubling because they can lead to a poorly timed decision. For this reason, before entering or exiting a position based on the appearance of either a northern or southern doji, you need to await confirmation.

The doji is a signal of a struggle between bulls and bears that equalizes between open and close for the session. However, given the frequency of its appearance, it is best to think of the doji as part of a larger pattern, as explained in previous chapters (notably in discussions about harasmi cross, doji star, and abandoned baby).

When the doji is combined with a gap within a pattern, it provides a very strong signal. This is called a *tri-star pattern*. A bull tri-star consists of three consecutive dojis with the middle one gapping below the first and third. A bear tri-star is the opposite: three consecutive dojis with the second gapping above the first and third. Consecutive doji sessions are rare, but finding three in a row with the applicable gap is even rarer. When you see this pattern, it is quite strong in the indicated direction. Figure 5-6 shows how the bull and bear tri-star appears.

📖 Tri-star

A pattern with three consecutive sessions showing dojis in each. A bull tri-star develops when the middle doji gaps below the ranges of the first and third sessions, and a bear tri-star consists of a second session gapping above the first and third.

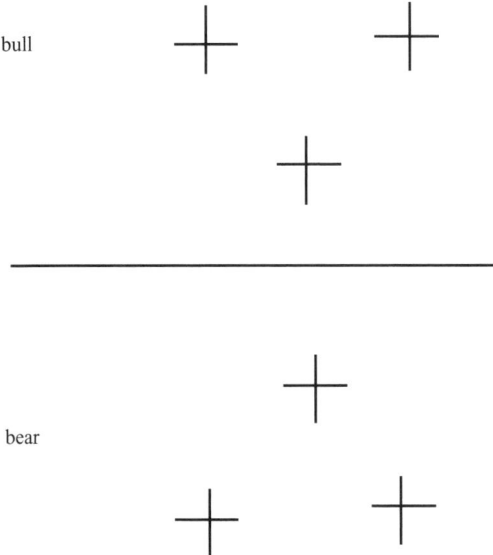

Figure 5-6 Tri-star patterns

The doji is a frequently recurring candle; however, the combination of consecutive sessions *and* double gaps is difficult to find. However, when it does it appear, it is a very strong signal. The identical (or close) open and close indicate a struggle between buyers and sellers, so the direction implied by the double gap makes the new direction more firmly established than in most reversal patterns.

Reversal Patterns with Gaps

Gaps serve a valuable function in reversal patterns. Gaps are exceptions to the "normal" trading pattern, in which a session's opening price is expected to exist within the trading range of the previous day. When this situation does not occur, it is wise to pay attention; a reversal could be underway. Many reversal patterns include gaps as part of the reversal.

✓ Key Point

Spotting reversals is not always easy. A key method is to look for gaps that also fit a reversal indicator. Gaps are exceptions and may foreshadow a change in direction.

A *kicking* pattern is the simplest formation; it consists of two consecutive sessions. As with the tri-star pattern, it is unusual to see the combination required for the kicking pattern. A bull kicking consists of a marubozu black session followed by an upward gap and a white candle; a bear pattern starts with a white marubozu and is followed by a downward gap and then a black candle. The marubozu is a candle with no upper or lower shadows. It opens at the low and closes at the high (white candle) or opens at the high and closes at the low (black candle). The bull and bear kicking patterns are shown in Figure 5-7.

📖 Kicking

A reversal pattern consisting of a marubozu, a gap above or below, and then a candle of the opposite color. A bull kicking starts with a black and ends with a white candle with an upside gap between the two, and a bear kicking starts with a white candle and ends with a black candle with a downside gap between the two.

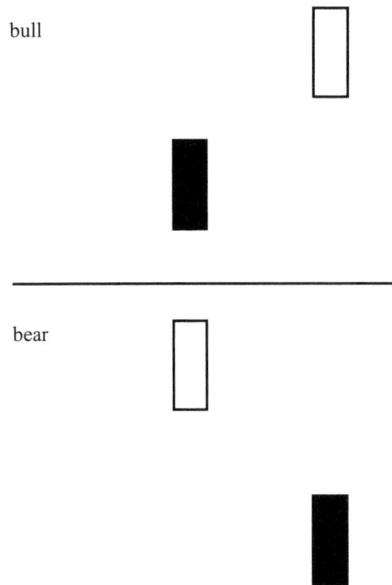

Figure 5-7 Kicking patterns

A second type of reversal with gaps included is called a *belt hold*. This pattern consists of three candles in a visible trend (three or more sessions with consecutive higher highs and higher lows in an uptrend, or with lower highs and lower lows in a downtrend), followed by a gap in the same direction and then a candle of the opposite color. The final candle should be white and have no lower shadow (bull belt hold) or black with no upper shadow (bear belt hold).

📖 Belt Hold

A reversal pattern consisting of three downtrend days, a downside gap, and a white candle with no lower shadow (bull); or three uptrend days, an upside gap, and a black candle with no upper shadow (bear).

A "perfect" belt hold is difficult to find, but a pattern coming close signals the bottoming out of a downtrend (in a bull pattern) or topping out (in a bear pattern). So the final entry may exhibit a small shadow and still qualify for this pattern. For example, Exxon Mobil (XOM) displayed a bull belt hold with a small shadow, as shown in Figure 5-8.

5 Reversal Pattern Analysis

Chart courtesy of StockCharts.com

Figure 5-8 Bull belt hold

The final candle has a slight lower shadow and the gap is small; even so, the pattern did accurately predict a reversal and uptrend, even though that uptrend was delayed by a few sessions. The bear belt hold, similarly, is not always perfect. The chart for Google (GOOG) makes this point in Figure 5-9.

Chart courtesy of StockCharts.com

Figure 5-9 Bear belt hold

> ✓ **Key Point**
>
> *Finding the perfect example of a particular reversal formation is rare. The important point to remember is that if the pattern contains most of the attributes and accurately predicts a reversal, it still counts.*

Even though this bear belt hold contained a small upper shadow in the final candle, it remained a very strong signal. It followed an uptrend consisting of eight sessions, the bear belt hold, and an immediate reversal lasting for nine sessions.

Reversals Setting New Support or Resistance

Although all reversal patterns rely on confirmation through other technical signs (strength or weakness of the reversal; for example, some patterns are based on establishing new resistance or support levels). The stronger the newly established support or resistance, the stronger the candle pattern.

A very strong bull reversal is a four-part pattern called the *concealing baby swallow*. This pattern involves four black candles. The first two are marubozus (candles with little or no shadows) with the second having lower open and close levels than the first. This is followed by a downside gap and a black candle; and fourth is a marubozu engulfing the third day's range. With such specific attributes, it is rare to find a perfect concealing baby swallow; however, patterns containing most of its features do establish the bottom of a downtrend and set a new support level.

📖 Concealing Baby Swallow

A bull reversal pattern consisting of four black candles; the first two are marubozus, followed by a downside gap, a third black candle, and then an engulfing black candle. This pattern sets a new support level for the trading range.

In Figure 5-10, McDonald's (MCD) showed a nearly complete concealing baby swallow with a double engulfing conclusion. The first two declining black candles were not perfect marubozu sticks. and a gap did not form. However, the engulfing attribute of the third and fourth candles was doubled, establishing a very strong support level.

Figure 5-10 Concealing baby swallow

Another descriptively named reversal pattern is the *stick sandwich*. This is a three-stick reversal with the middle stick a different color than the first and thirds. The bull stick sandwich starts with a black stick and then a middle white stick. Finally, another black stick appears with a closing price the same as the first. This establishes a new support level, based on the premise that sellers were unable to drive the price lower than that level; it may precede a long-standing support level and a strong bull trend in the stock.

✓ Key Point

The stick sandwich is aptly named because the middle candle is the opposite color of the candles on either side.

📖 Stick Sandwich

A reversal three-stick pattern in which the first and third sticks are one color and the middle the opposite color. The closing prices of the first and third sticks are at the same level, establishing new support (bull) or new resistance (bear) price levels.

For example, JCPenney (JCP) revealed a bull stick sandwich at the bottom of a downtrend, as shown in Figure 5-11. The newly established support level was tested and then a strong and long-term uptrend began.

Chart courtesy of StockCharts.com

Figure 5-11 Bull stick sandwich

The bear stick sandwich has opposite attributes: the first and third candles are white; and the middle, black. The closing prices of the first and third are identical, setting up a new resistance level. For example, in Figure 5-12, Chevron Corp (CVX) experienced a bear stick sandwich after a pause in a downtrend, setting new resistance and then falling once again. This interim example is not perfect, but it does demonstrate how the resistance level can be reestablished by this pattern.

Figure 5-12 Bear stick sandwich

A more basic version of the stick sandwich is found in the more readily spotted *matching* move. In this two-stick formation, the closing price is identical on two consecutive days with the same color candlestick. A bull move, the matching low, consists of two black candles with the same close, setting up new support; and a bear move, the matching high, is made up of two white candles with matching closing prices, establishing new resistance.

📖 Matching Pattern

A bull reversal move consisting of two black candles with identical closing prices (matching low), establishing a new support level; or a bear reversal with two white candles with identical closing prices (matching high), establishing a new resistance level.

For example, United Technologies (UTX) had both types of matching moves, shown in Figure 5-13. First, a matching high developed, setting a new resistance level and preceding a start downtrend. Second was a matching bottom, setting a new support level and followed by an even longer uptrend. Although this two-stick move is subtle, it does not appear frequently and is a valuable indicator that, once confirmed, anticipates a strong reversal.

Figure 5-13 Matching moves

> ✓ **Key Point**
>
> The matching move is rare, but when you see it, there is a strong likelihood of a reversal; this signal is especially strong.

The concepts of resistance and support are core attributes in the price trend, making these patterns very reliable. They do not occur frequently, but when they do, they provide strong evidence of reversal. The more conforming the patterns to all the attributes they involve, the stronger the value of the signal.

More Resistance and Support Reversals

Variations of previously introduced patterns add great value to reversal analysis. For example, the three black crows pattern (consecutive black sticks moving downward) is usually bearish. In one subtle variation of this pattern, the opposite indication applies. Awareness of this important distinction can help avoid acting on a false indicator.

5 Reversal Pattern Analysis

The pattern called *three stars in the south* appears at the bottom of a downtrend and anticipates a reversal. It looks like the three black crows but contains some distinct differences. All three sessions are black. The first has a long lower shadow. The second has a smaller trading range with a low close below the close of the first candle. The third is a small black marubozu lying within the trading range of the second candle.

📖 Three Stars in the South

A bull reversal consisting of three black candles. The first has a long lower shadow, the second closes lower, and the third is a marubozu with a range within the range of the second session.

For example, Yahoo! (YHOO) revealed a pattern that was almost a perfect three stars in the south. The final candle was not a marubozu, but it was close. Most significant was the establishment of a new support level, highlighted on Figure 5-14. The extension of the bottom trading range of the three sticks is a perfect demonstration of what the three stars in the south should display: black candles with rising lower shadow extensions, giving a strong indication of a reversal.

Chart courtesy of StockCharts.com

Figure 5-14   Three stars in the south

Like the three stars pattern, the *three rivers pattern* sets new support (bottom) or resistance (top). The bull pattern (three rivers bottom) consists of a long black candle followed by a black candle whose range is lower than the first and with its lower shadow setting a new low, and then a short white candle closing lower than the second day's close.

📖 Three Rivers Pattern

A reversal formation consisting of a long black candle, a lower black and a short white candle closing lower (three rivers bottom, a bull formation); or a long white candle, a white higher candle, and a short black candle closing higher (three rivers top, a bear formation).

For example, Disney (DIS) showed a very strong three rivers bottom containing all the required attributes, as shown in Figure 5-15. The pattern set a new support level, which was followed by a very strong uptrend.

Chart courtesy of StockCharts.com

Figure 5-15 Three rivers bottom

The bear pattern (three rivers top) consists of a long white candle followed by a white candle with a higher range and with its upper shadow setting a new high, and then a short black candle closing higher than the second day's close.

✓ Key Point

Reversal patterns that establish new resistance or support are especially reliable. The new trading border confirms the pattern and occurs most often at the beginning of the reversal.

A three rivers top was found in the chart of JCPenney (JCP), shown in Figure 5-16. This topping pattern is exceptionally strong, not only because of the strong three rivers formation but also because volume spiked on the setup day as well. Heavier-than-usual volume is one of the "red flags" of impending reversal. In the case of the bear reversal, high volume combined with the long upward session indicates that buying interest is becoming exhausted. The ensuring downtrend confirms this conclusion.

Figure 5-16 Three rivers top

The preceding subtle patterns all set resistance and support and may be difficult to spot in an emerging chart. When combined with other technical indicators and confirmed, candlestick reversals that strongly set or reset these resistance and support levels are highly reliable.

Multisession Gap Reversals

Some reversal patterns extend beyond the common three-session span and four sessions or longer. The more complex *breakaway pattern* has a gap that is filled several sessions after it is set up.

📖 Breakaway Pattern

A reversal pattern in which the first candle is followed by a gap in the direction established (downward for a black candle or upward for a white candle). A series of the same-colored candles follows moving in the same direction, concluding with a candle of the opposite color closing into the gap (upward for a bull breakaway or downward for a bear breakaway).

The bull breakaway's trading sessions involves

- *First session:* A long black candle (followed by a downward gap)
- *Second and third sessions (or more):* Consecutively lower closes and all black candles
- *Last session:* A long white candle closing into the gap

An example of a bull breakaway is Exxon Mobil (XOM), as shown in Figure 5-17. The final session (white) closes into the downward gap previously set and precedes a strong upward reversal.

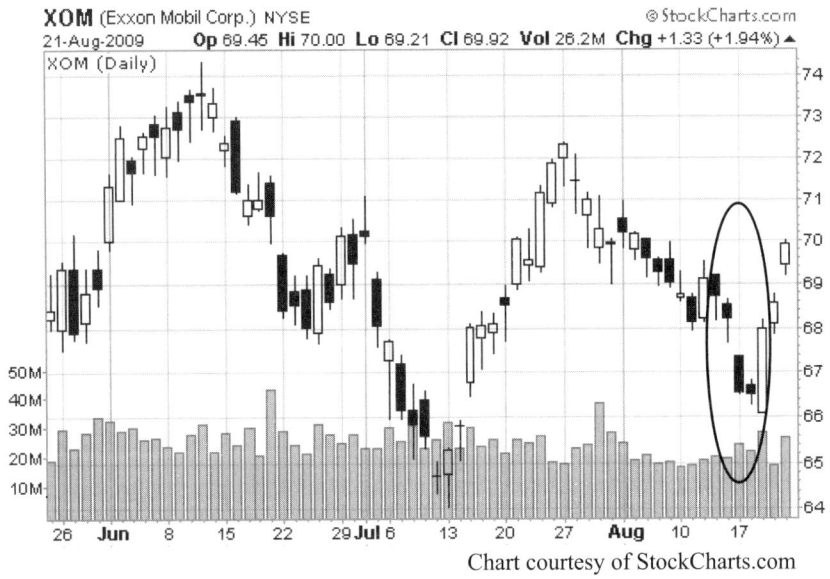

Chart courtesy of StockCharts.com

Figure 5-17   Bull breakaway

A bear breakaway moves in the opposite direction. Figure 5-18 demonstrates this in the case of Boeing (BA). This is a strong reversal, following a quick uptrend and predicting an equally quick downtrend.

Reversal Pattern Analysis 113

Figure 5-18   Bear breakaway

The *mat hold* is a bull reversal with a gap setting new support. More than three sessions are involved:

- *First session:* A long white candle (followed by an upside gap)
- *Second session:* A black session
- *Third and fourth sessions:* Black candles moving lower and into the range of the first day, closing the gap
- *Last session:* A long white session closing above the price of the first session

📖 Mat Hold

A bull reversal pattern beginning with a long white candle, followed by an upside gap, downward black candles, and a final white candle closing higher than the first candle.

For example, the chart for Pfizer (PFE) revealed a modified version of this pattern, as shown in Figure 5-19. This example is not perfect, but it does approximate the trend that sets new support. The indicated series of candles is interrupted, but the support level is established (with immediate high prices tested) and precedes a strong uptrend.

Figure 5-19 Mat hold

A bear version of the pattern is called the *falling three pattern*. In this formation, you find the following series:

- *First session:* A long black candle (followed by a downside gap)
- *Second session:* A white session
- *Third and fourth sessions:* White candles moving higher and into the range of the first day, closing the gap
- *Last session:* A long black session closing below the price of the first session

Falling Three Pattern

A bear reversal pattern and the opposite of the bull reversal mat hold. This pattern consists of a black session, a downside gap, a series of rising white sessions, and a final black session closing lower than the close of the first. This pattern sets a new resistance level and anticipates a downtrend.

An example of this trend, setting a new resistance level, was found in the chart of Exxon Mobil (XOM), shown in Figure 5-20. In this instance, the pattern appears *after* the uptrend topped out rather than at the exact top. In addition, there are only two middle sessions rather than three. In many cases, a "perfect" pattern is not possible, but the overall formation and what it anticipates are more significant. When you are studying a current trend that appears to have topped out and paused, how do you know whether the uptrend will continue or reverse? This is where the emergence of a reversal signal is helpful. This newly established resistance level precedes a strong downtrend.

> ✓ **Key Point**
>
> *Reversal patterns that follow brief periods of sideways trading are valuable as long as they signal a reversal of the previous direction. This helps to decide when sideways trading is coming to an end.*

Chart courtesy of StockCharts.com

Figure 5-20 Falling three pattern

A variation on the theme of black candles signaling a reversal to an uptrend (or white candles anticipating a downtrend) is found in the *ladder pattern*. This series concludes with a gap right before the turn.

📖 Ladder Pattern

A reversal pattern beginning with a series of candles trending in one direction, a gap in the opposite direction, and a candle that moves in the reversal direction. A ladder bottom (black candles, an upside gap, and a higher white session) is a bull reversal, and a ladder top (white candles, a downside gap, and a black session) is a bear reversal.

An example of a ladder bottom is shown in the chart for Google (GOOG), shown in Figure 5-21. The pattern sets new support, but this support is immediately tested with a double bottom falling below that level, before the anticipated uptrend takes over. In the ideal ladder bottom, the final black candle before the gap should have an upper shadow and little or no lower shadow. In this instance, the stronger upper shadow makes a convincing argument that this is a legitimate ladder bottom.

Chart courtesy of StockCharts.com

Figure 5-21 Ladder bottom

The bear version, the ladder top, contains the same pattern but with opposite colors. For example, DuPont (DD) experienced a ladder bottom, shown in Figure 5-22. The final white candle ideally should reveal a strong lower shadow, which is absent in this situation. Even so, new resistance is established and a downtrend does follow as expected.

5 Reversal Pattern Analysis

Figure 5-22 Ladder top

The many variations of reversal patterns are exceptionally valuable timing mechanisms, but must also be confirmed by other technical indicators or accepted only when the pattern is exceptionally strong. The many variables (long candles, marubozu formation, presence of upper and lower shadows, the expanse of gaps, and the extension of the preceding trend) all provide good intelligence about how strong the reversal signal is likely to be, and of course, this also anticipates how strongly the trend will occur once direction has been reversed.

> ✓ **Key Point**
>
> *Reversal signals, by themselves, are useful but never tell the whole story. When combined with traditional technical analysis, they vastly improve your timing for entry and exit from positions.*

Combining specific reversal patterns with traditional technical indicators is an excellent system for building confirmation and also for getting an advance indication that a reversal is underway. For this reason, building skills in chart analysis improves your ability to spot reversals as well as false reversals. The next chapter expands on the importance of candlestick pattern recognition by tying in two important additional pieces of information: volume and volatility.

chapter 6

Volume and Volatility

In addition to price movement and pattern, volume of trading and volatility (risk) are also valuable indicators. Focusing solely on price trends is a mistake because changes in volume indicate changes in trading activity, and such changes often accompany or even anticipate changes in price trends. The same is true for changes in volatility levels; broadening trading ranges or repeated violations of support or resistance indicate coming price changes.

Candlestick chart patterns are powerful price monitoring tools. When combined with the equally important volume and volatility signs, candlesticks are even more effective. Changes in volume and volatility can also confirm what price patterns imply about impending trends.

Volume as a Price Indicator

Movement in price and changes in daily volume are separate matters. However, volume also serves as a key price indicator, especially when studied in conjunction with significant candlestick formations accompanied by unusual spikes in volume levels. Candlestick charts are normally presented with volume in histogram bar form on the bottom of the chart; the charts used in this book include these volume levels, with the daily level (in numbers of shares traded) shown on the bottom left of the chart.

> ✓ **Key Point**
> Although volume and price are separate from one another, volume may serve as an important confirming indicator, especially in reversal formations.

As a general rule, volume is most useful when compared to daily price candlestick formations. Devices such as moving averages of volume are not particularly useful for most traders because, unlike price trends, volume trends are easily distorted by a few spikes. These volume spikes may have little to do with a *trend* in volume itself, so moving averages are more useful in price trends. When volume increases steadily from one day to the next, the trend serves as confirmation of a developing price trend. The confirming aspect of volume as it accompanies a price move is the best application of volume analysis.

Volume also confirms a trend when changes accompany price breakouts. Support and resistance are the "lines in the sand" for technicians, and breakouts are among the strongest of technical signals. However, some breakouts are the beginning of a strong trend resulting in a new price range, and other breakouts are aberrations, after which price levels will return to previously set levels. How do you know which is which? The answer often is found when a breakout is accompanied by heavy volume. This is especially likely to work as confirmation that the breakout is permanent when it follows a period of price consolidation and low volume. In an upside breakout such as this, the indication is particularly strong because an influx of new buyers supports the higher price range. In a downside breakout, heavy volume can also be significant, but it is not necessary to justify lower prices. The momentum of a resistance breakout is going to be the most important attribute of the trend and the determining factor to its permanent or temporary nature. The same momentum is not as crucial for a support breakout.

After a strong upside breakout with higher-than-typical volume, a fast retreat in volume levels can work as a sign of exhaustion in new buyer interest. This can anticipate a price retreat. At such times, watching candlestick patterns and exercising caution are wise ideas. The use of trailing stops or taking of some profits is advisable whenever resistance breakouts occur, but especially if volume levels retreat immediately after the breakouts occurs. Remember, though, that higher-than-average volume is not going to be sustained indefinitely. Even in a strong price movement, volume levels are going to subside. The point here is that an immediate retreat after an upside breakout can be a warning sign.

✓ Key Point

Spikes in volume are rarely permanent, and in a majority of cases volume will return within one to two sessions to previously established levels.

For example, in the case of Travelers (TRV), a breakout was followed by a quick retreat of a single-day volume spike. After this, prices did retreat back into the past trading range. This scenario is shown in Figure 6-1.

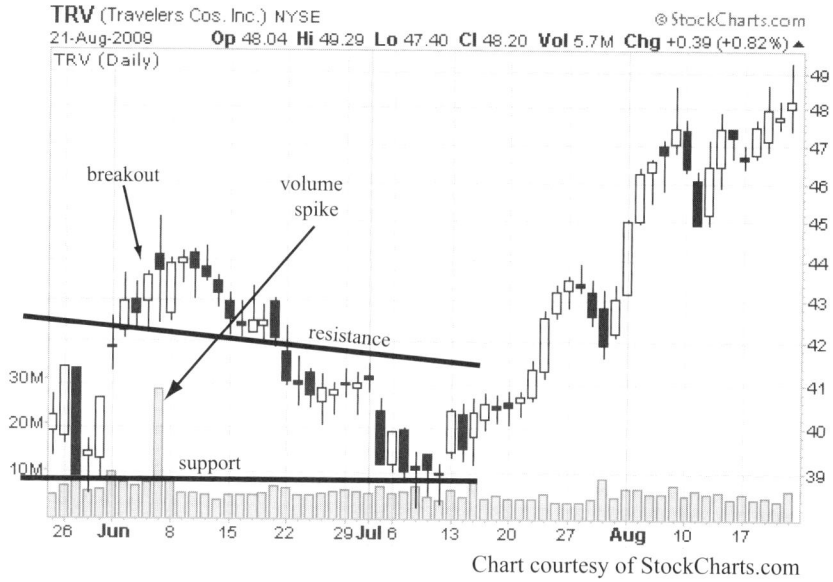

Figure 6-1 Retreating volume trend

This example makes the point that a single-day spike in volume accompanying a breakout above resistance could signal that it is not going to last. The immediate retreat in volume was quickly accompanied by a retreat in price as well. However, volume by itself is not a reliable indicator of changes in the trading range. Note that subsequently, the price levels for Travelers did rise—and significantly—without any discernable changes in volume. From this outcome, you can conclude that when you see changes in volume, the changes can be interpreted based on whether higher volume remains or immediately falls away. However, the volume trend as a confirming factor is not going to be apparent in every instance.

It is equally as likely that price breakouts will occur with no "red flag" changes in volume. The extra confirming value of higher volume is useful, but is not always there. For example, a strong price breakout in Cisco (CSCO) occurred without any big changes in daily volume. This trend is shown in Figure 6-2.

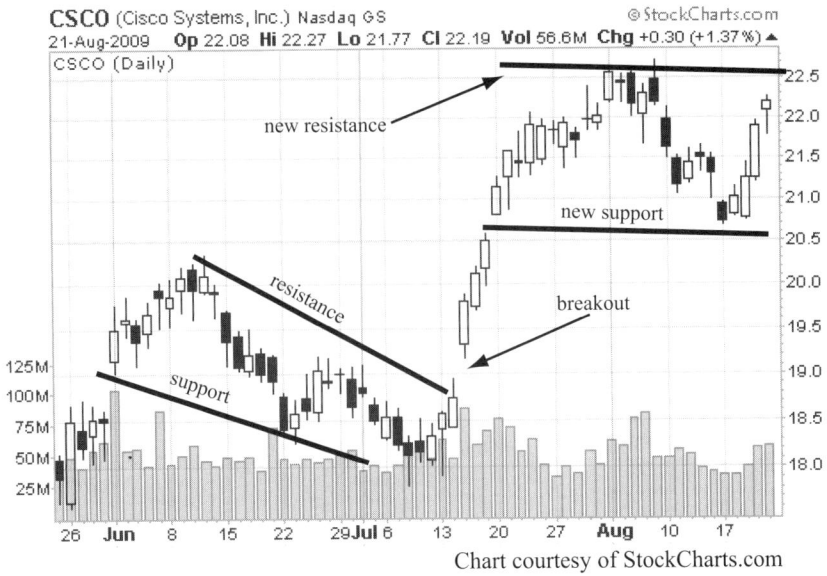

Figure 6-2 Breakout with no volume spike

In any analysis of volume, the price pattern witnessed in the candlestick is the most important attribute of a trend, reversal, or breakout pattern. Volume is a useful form of confirmation as well as a method for judging the strength of the pattern.

Volume Indicators

Observing a spike in daily volume is only the most apparent of the useful confirmation signals volume can provide. A number of useful technical indicators based on volume and volume trends further aid in rounding out a candlestick-based price analysis program.

Many volume-based indicators are valuable in conjunction with known candlestick chart patterns. These are less obvious than price movement because price is visible on charts. The causes for increases or decreases in volume are not always as apparent as the reasons for price trends and reversals. However, volume-based indicators can provide needed confirmation for what you observe in the candlestick formations. Confusing the issue is the dominance of institutional trading. Large volume is not always a reliable signal of a change in buyer or seller sentiment about a company. It might also be the result of one or more large mutual funds taking positions or selling shares. This situation often occurs near the end of a reporting period, when fund management wants to clean up its portfolio to present a positive picture to shareholders. Thus, a block of shares may be sold just before the end of a quarter to take profits, or a block might be sold right after the end of the quarter to report losses at the beginning of the next quarter.

> ✓ **Key Point**
>
> *Exceptionally high volume might have no actual significance, especially if it occurs near the end of the quarter. It might be caused by institutional investor changes in their portfolio mix.*

The timing among institutional investors—which account for up to 75 or 80 percent of all shares held in many companies—can distort the picture of what is going on with a company and its stock. With this in mind, any time you observe a spike in volume, also check the proximity of the date to the end of the month, and proceed with caution.

Perhaps one of the most interesting volume trends is anticipation of a price move. If you see volume gradually increasing, indicating growing interest in the stock on the upside, or growing concerns on the downside, check candlestick patterns to determine whether volume in that case is acting as a leading indicator of price trend. This signal is especially strong when accompanied by equally important candlestick signs or moves. Check the chart for MMM, shown in Figure 6-3.

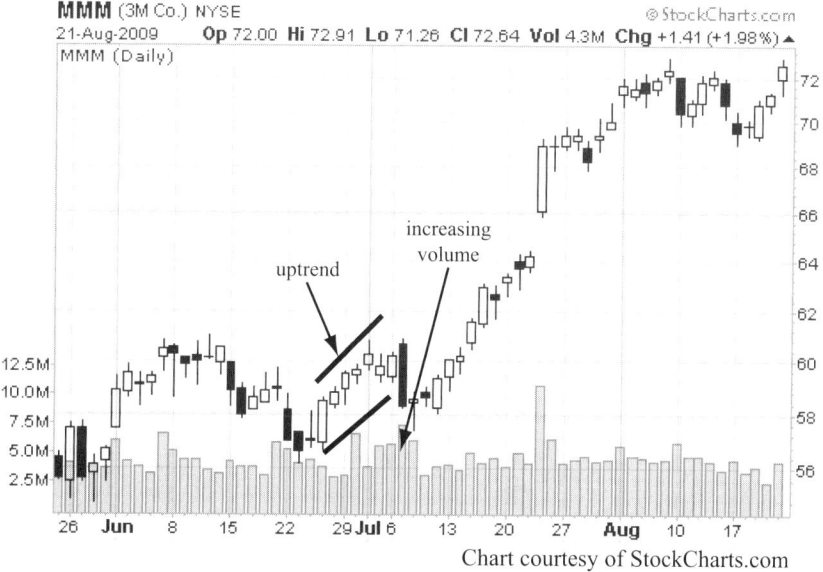

Chart courtesy of StockCharts.com

Figure 6-3 Volume as a leading indicator

This pattern is interesting in several ways. The uptrend concludes with a very prominent black marubozu. This is most often thought of as a reversal sign when it appears during a downtrend. But when it is seen in conjunction with an uptrend, it can also act as a continuation signal. This is true in the case of MMM. The black marubozu is also called a *major yin*.

📖 Major Yin

A black marubozu sign serving as a reversal sign within a downtrend or, when it appears within an uptrend, as a continuation indicator.

The MMM chart is also interesting because of the exceptionally strong breakout above resistance. Every chartist knows that a breakout can reverse and price can retreat back into the range, or it can continue. In this instance, price not only continues upward; a few sessions after the volume-led uptrend, volume again peaks while the price gaps upward, moving price even higher. Both of these trend movements are accompanied by very meaningful changes in volume. However, they take on the meaning only when accompanied by the important candlestick patterns as well. These patterns include the uptrend in the initial move, the black marubozu, and the price gap in the second phase. That last movement is an exhaustion gap, preceding a newly established trading range between $68 and $73 per share.

The uptrend reinforced with a black marubozu is very unusual. A more commonly observed volume trend is on-balance volume and money flow indicators of several kinds. As with other technical indicators, these should be used as confirmation of candlestick patterns and trends, and not as primary determining factors in timing of buy and sell orders. *On-balance volume* is an idea first proposed by the well-known market bull Joseph Granville. In his view, this was a condition in which neither buyers nor sellers controlled price movement. As one side or the other begins to dominate volume, it implies an emerging trend. The analysis of volume is maintained on a cumulative basis to make this analysis work. When either the buyers or the sellers tip the on-balance in one direction or the other, it signals an emerging trend in that direction as well.

📖 On-balance Volume

A cumulative indicator measuring dominance of daily trading by either buyers or sellers, used to anticipate emerging trends.

On-balance volume is an effective method for quantifying volume-based price trends. A problem with it, however, is that volume is always mixed. However, in spite of how closely aligned buyers and sellers actually are, even a slight edge moves the entire day into one column or the other. This move potentially distorts the trend itself. For this reason, anyone analyzing candlestick pricing trends should use on-balance volume as one of many ways to double-check and confirm a trend implied by candlestick movement; relying on the on-balance volume as a sole indicator or even as the primary signal may lead to some ill-timed decisions.

✓ Key Point

On-balance volume is a useful but imperfect indicator. If a day's volume is closely mixed between buyers and sellers, even a slight edge will throw the entire day's volume into one column or the other.

An expansion of volume analysis is the indicator known as *money flow*. This variation of volume analysis uses an average of high, low, and close for each day to calculate volume trend. Compared to the on-balance volume using closing price alone, money flow is more precise.

📖 Money Flow

A technical test of volume trends employing the average of each day's high, low, and close to develop a cumulative trend direction in price.

Both on-balance volume and money flow should be used with caution and always in conjunction with candlestick pattern analysis. However, one of the interesting aspects of volume trend analysis is divergence. When you uncover positive money flow while stock prices are falling, or negative money flow while prices are in an uptrend, what does this flow signal?

Divergence is going to occur in even the most accurate and reliable tests, whether based on daily cumulative levels of "ownership" of volume by either buyers or sellers, long-term moving averages, or other adjustments meant to eliminate spikes. This drawback to volume analysis led to two refinements, both developed by Marc Chaikin. His two major contributions to technical analysis were the accumulation/distribution (AD) indicator and money flow index (MFI).

📖 Accumulation/Distribution (AD)

A technical indicator measuring proportionate degrees of buyer and seller volume, which acts as a momentum indicator.

The A/D indicator is calculated with a specific formula:

(((closing price - low price) - (high price - closing price)) ÷ (high price - low price)) × volume = A/D

This indicator makes volume analysis more accurate that on-balance volume. Assignment of a day's volume as controlled by either buyers or sellers is more accurate after calculating the mean of prices for each day. The resulting A/D indicator is either +1 or -1. Chaikin also devised the money flow index (MFI), which measures the strength of money flow in a stock's price. This indicator should not be confused with the earlier explained money flow; the MFI tracks money flow over a 21-day moving average, identifying positive (buyer) and negative (seller) flow and their net difference. This indicator identifies the longer-term momentum in price trend.

📖 Money Flow Index (MFI)

A momentum indicator measuring positive and negative money flow in a stock's price over a 21-day moving average, creating an oscillator ranging between 1 and 100; the indicator is also known as the Chaikin Money Flow (CMF).

✓ Key Point

The MFI is a preferred measurement of volume because it is based on a moving average and trend, and because the trend reflects the net change over time between buyer and seller dominance.

Positive flow is divided by negative flow to develop each day's entry into the MFI trend, and the result is multiplied by 100. An oscillator below 20 indicates that the stock is then oversold, acting as a buy signal. When the oscillator rises above 80, the opposite conclusion results: the stock is overbought and this behavior serves as a sell signal. MFI has a great advantage over most other volume-based price indicators because it is very easy to follow.

Volume Indicators and Candlesticks

The value of volume-based price indicators is apparent to the dedicated chartist, who knows that all indicators can serve to confirm continuation of a trend or provide early warnings of impending reversal, or to contradict other signs. For example, although candlestick moves and patterns provide strong signals, they are not always timely or even correct. This is where on-balance volume and the Chaikin Money Flow (CMF) are valuable. Combining these indicators as part of a price trend analysis based on candlesticks can improve timing and bolster an initial indicator.

The purpose here is not to provide an in-depth analysis of higher-level technical indicators, but to demonstrate how they provide insight into the trend itself, and how you can more readily anticipate the gradual weakening or strengthening of the trend over time. Fortunately for anyone who wants the data available but does not want to develop moving averages, modern charting available online and free of charge includes any number of technical indicators as additions to charts. This makes their availability instantaneous. A study of candlestick trends along with a short list of volume indicators is especially wise. Limiting the analysis to only two indicators makes sense because if you include too many, you can easily become lost in the complexity of interpreting all of them.

Combining two indicators (on-balance volume and CMF) is a good place to start. No single indicator can reveal all that you need to know, and decisions should not be made based on a sole candlestick, or on a sole volume-based trend. In an ideal world, you expect to see all indicators pointing to the same conclusion; in reality, of course, you often find serious contradictions between the indicators you trust. In analyzing the CMF, you look for three attributes to indicate what is going on in the current trend:

1. *Is the CMF positive or negative?* Regardless of how price is acting, remember that the money flow is a moving average, and this accurately pegs a positive (bullish) or negative (bearish) trend underway.

2. *How long has the current situation prevailed?* The longer the CMF remains either positive or negative, the stronger the related trend. This information is especially valuable in highly volatile markets, where price ranges have broadened and longer-term price trends have become more difficult to spot.

3. *How strong is the CMF status?* The intensity of the indicator is also a key ingredient in its interpretation. As a general rule, when the oscillator is at 0.10, it is bullish (or when -0.10, it is bearish). When the oscillator moves to 0.25, it is extremely bullish, and at -0.25, it is extremely bearish. These extremes identify the likely tops and bottoms of price trends and are among the strongest of confirming signals. However, these extremes do not always appear, so rather than waiting for them, you should treat them as exceptional signals rather than signals necessary to make a move.

Some charting examples make the point concerning the use of technical indicators along with candlestick moves and patterns. In these instances, six-month charts have been used in place of three-month charts used elsewhere. This approach helps to show a longer-term development of technical volume trends. The first is the chart for American Express (AXP), which is shown in Figure 6-4.

Figure 6-4 Bullish volume indicator

> ✓ **Key Point**
>
> In a sustained uptrend, it is difficult to identify the right time to sell and take profits. This is where the CMF oscillator can be valuable and help spot whether the trend is ending or continuing.

In this chart, the long-standing and exceptional uptrend creates a dilemma. When should you sell and take profits? Many analysts, looking only at the candlestick moves and patterns, might note the black marubozu at the start of September as a reversal signal, notably because the CMF dipped below zero at the same time, or the narrow-range day in mid-November as another indicator that the uptrend was ending. In both cases, the candlestick indicators were not enough by themselves to cause a sell signal. In the most recent CMF, the oscillator rose above 0.25 for the first time in three months. This outcome indicates that, rather than moving toward a weakening of the trend, it is time to hold or even increase a position in this stock. On-balance volume has remained consistently high throughout the period as well.

The AXP chart supports holding shares rather than selling and taking profits. A different scenario is found in the chart of Alcoa (AA). Here, a more bearish conclusion is reached based on a combined analysis of the candlestick patterns, on-balance volume, and CMF. This example is shown in Figure 6-5.

Figure 6-5 Bearish volume indicator

This chart, like the previous one, shows a very bearish move and a marubozu with very little tail. This is a strong bear sign in the candlestick alone. Augmenting this indicator is on-balance volume, which has leveled out in recent weeks, showing that on a daily volume basis, neither buyers nor sellers were in control. The most revealing signal, however, is the CMF. Note the decline in the oscillator and its fall to below -0.25 at one point near the end of the chart. This foreshadows a price decline. Given the 50 percent increase in price levels since the past July level, this is the time to take profits, based on the candlestick pattern and the on-balance and CMF confirmation.

A third chart shows how the volume-based indicators can contradict the apparent price trend. The chart of DuPont (DD), in Figure 6-6, reveals a decline CMF indicator even while price levels remain higher than in the recent past.

Chart courtesy of StockCharts.com

Figure 6-6   Contradictory volume indicator

This situation is troubling. Price—viewed by itself—seems to be moving upward. At the same time, on-balance volume confirms this movement, but the CMF is moving strongly in the opposite direction. If we look at how price acts subsequently, the positive trend continues; however, the CMF is sustaining its negative posture. One of the three attributes of CMF—duration of status—should dominate in this condition. The combination of signals, while confusing due to the contradiction, is bearish. In this situation buyers are likely to be unable to sustain the current price levels. A retreat is likely in the near future. As an indicator and not a guarantee, this is only one possible interpretation. However, given the importance of CMF and its persistent bearish level, a prudent move at this point would be to sell or to employ trailing stops to prevent some portion of loss in the event of a sudden and strong price correction.

✓ Key Point

The duration of a volume indicator like CMF helps you to decipher otherwise contradictory signs. How long has the CMF remained in positive or negative territory?

Testing Price Volatility

Volume tests serve as confirmation for what you observe in the candlestick signs, moves, and patterns. They also help you spot changing directions in a trend as early as possible. However, volume is only half of the noncandlestick confirmation test. The other half is volatility, or the degree and scope of change in a stock's price.

Price volatility is the major symptom of market risk. The greater the price volatility, the higher your market risk. This risk is going to manifest in two ways. First is a broadening trading range over time; second is a tendency for price to bounce between resistance and support in larger increments and more frequently than in the past. In the technical sense, risk is based on the volatility of price and a real or perceived weakness in price support. Thus, a strong support level is perceived as a safety net. By the same argument, a weak support level or one that is violated with price decline is a symptom of high-risk stock positions. For the technician, this technically based market risk is the most serious consideration in picking stocks. However, it is wise to also be aware of fundamentally based market risk and how that affects price trends.

The fundamental market risk is going to be manifested in price volatility, either as a lagging indicator or—more often—preceding actual price trend changes. This is seen in many forms:

1. *Traditional form of fundamental volatility.* The tendency for a company to report volatile revenue and earnings makes it very difficult to predict long-term trends. So when profits are high one year and low the next, followed by a year of jarring net losses, how can you predict the future? This most basic version of fundamental volatility has the most direct correlation to technical price volatility.

2. *P/E-caused volatility.* If the P/E ratio tends to rise over time, it is also likely that prices are going to react with growing volatility. A moderate-range P/E—between 10 and 20, for example—is viewed by many as a reasonable expectation and one of many ways to reduce a list of trading candidates. Once P/E rises above this moderate range, the stock becomes too expensive. A bear might use high-P/E stocks for short positions, but most traders prefer to make long plays on lower-P/E stocks.

3. *Subtle cause and effect.* A few key fundamental tests have a direct effect on price volatility, although this often is a delayed effect. Among the most important are changes in dividend yield, debt ratio, and declining net return. The dividend yield is a sound method for judging management's cash flow control and growth plans, debt ratio identifies companies overly dependent on debt, and the net return is a key ratio even the ardent technician recognizes as crucial in stock picking. This is especially true when revenue is on the rise but net return is declining. This effect could be a symptom of decreasing internal controls and management effectiveness.

> ✓ **Key Point**
> *Even if you believe completely in technical analysis, also keep an eye on the fundamentals. Price volatility is likely to reflect changes in financial condition, which in turn changes the stock's market risk.*

Generally speaking, fundamental indicators are not viewed as having an immediate impact on price volatility. Even so, in picking one stock over another, price patterns and trends are not the sole way to determine likely trading candidates. Testing volatility also makes sense.

Rather than trying to measure and quantify volatility using one of many formulas, it is more valuable to visualize the trading range and observe consistency in breadth, or an expanding or narrowing trend in that range. Two patterns—*triangles* and *wedges*—are valuable in recognizing changes in volatility over time.

📖 Triangles

Continuation patterns characterized by a narrowing trading range over time; they may be symmetrical, ascending, or descending.

There are three types of triangle patterns, all reflecting continuation of the trend by way of a narrowing trading range. First is the *symmetrical triangle*, which is also called a *coil*. In this pattern, a triangle forms with at least two lower highs and two higher lows, followed by continuation of the established trend with approximately the same breadth as that in the beginning of the triangle.

📖 Symmetrical Triangle

A continuation pattern consisting of a trading range of the same breadth in both the beginning of the triangle and the continuation.

📖 Coil

Alternate name for the symmetrical triangle.

An example of this triangle is found twice in the six-month chart for Microsoft (MSFT). This example is shown in Figure 6-7.

In both instances, the direction is bullish, and the short-lived symmetrical triangle was followed by more upward movement in price. Both also conform to the uniformity of breadth. At the beginning of the first triangle, trading breadth was three points (from $22.00 to $25.00 per share). At the end of the triangle and continuation of the trend, the range remained at three points (from $22.50 to $25.50). The second symmetrical triangle repeated with a 2.5-point breadth. At the beginning of the triangle, range was between $24.50 and $27.00 per share; at the continuation point it was between $26.00 and $28.50.

Chart courtesy of StockCharts.com

Figure 6-7 Symmetrical triangle pattern

✓ Key Point

The symmetrical triangle is one of the strongest confirming patterns when the candlestick indicators are in question. Confirmation of the existing direction is as important as the more easily spotted reversal signal.

The symmetrical pattern is a clear continuation, and it is found in both bullish and bearish trends. In comparison, other types of triangles are either bullish or bearish based on their shape. The *ascending triangle* is a bullish pattern consisting of a consistent price level at resistance and a rising support level.

📖 Ascending Triangle

A bullish triangle characterized by a level resistance and rising support level.

For example, the six-month chart for Bank of America (BAC) provides an example of the ascending triangle. This triangle is shown in Figure 6-8.

Chart courtesy of StockCharts.com

Figure 6-8 Ascending triangle pattern

The pattern precedes a strong continuation of the uptrend. The same rule works in a bearish trend. The *descending triangle* contains a steady level of support with declining resistance. An example is found in the six-month chart of Verizon (VZ), shown in Figure 6-9.

📖 Descending Triangle

A bearish continuation pattern consisting of steady support price and declining resistance.

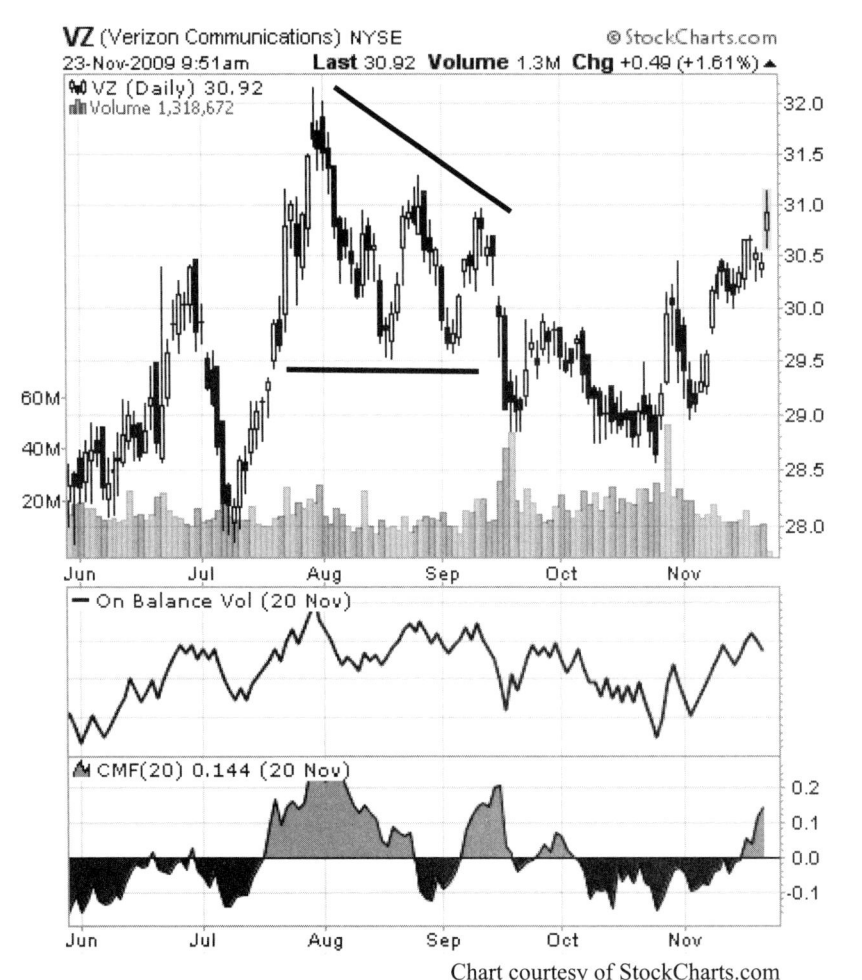

Chart courtesy of StockCharts.com

Figure 6-9 Descending triangle pattern

Like the continuation patterns of triangles, *wedges* are reversal patterns characterized by narrowing trading range. A rising wedge is bearish, and a falling wedge is bullish.

📖 Wedge

A reversal pattern in one of two shapes: a rising wedge is bearish, anticipating a reversal from the existing uptrend to a downtrend; and a falling wedge is bullish, anticipating a reversal from the existing downtrend to an uptrend.

A *rising wedge* is bearish because, although prices are moving, their narrowing (wedge) formation anticipates a coming price decline. An example is found in the six-month chart of Best Buy (BBY), as shown in Figure 6-10.

Chart courtesy of StockCharts.com

Figure 6-10 Rising wedge pattern

📖 Rising Wedge

A reversal pattern in which prices rise while the price range narrows, anticipating a coming price decline.

Although this example is minimal in size, the pattern is true. The rising price with narrowing range anticipates a coming price decline. In comparison, a *falling wedge* anticipates a reversal to the upside and is considered a bullish pattern.

📖 Falling Wedge

A reversal pattern in which prices fall while the price range narrows, anticipating a coming price rise.

✓ Key Point

A wedge does not have to be extreme to properly identify a coming reversal. Many examples prove that even a slight wedge movement is adequate to foreshadow the change.

For example, the six-month chart for Alcoa (AA) provides a good example of a falling wedge. This wedge is shown in Figure 6-11.

There are two falling wedges on the chart, highlighted by the resistance and support lines. In both cases, the reversal holds and prices rise after the narrowing breadth occurs.

In all the triangle and wedge examples, changes in the breadth of the trading range define either continuation or reversal. These examples of volatility as a confirming indicator with candlestick analysis are most useful when reviewed in line with other technical signals (such as on-balance volume and CMF) and, most of all, to verify and confirm candlestick moves and patterns.

Any charting system, including candlesticks, is going to put forth false signals on occasion. The value in developing and employing a system is not to eliminate errors, but to reduce them. The result, making well-timed decisions more often, is the desirable outcome. Analysis based on both volume and volatility is valuable because it provides additional confirmation to signals you pick up from observing candlestick signs, moves, and patterns. Spotting weakening trends or continuation signals may clarify what short-term candlestick patterns reveal or seem to reveal. Significant signs like marubozu days may get your attention initially; any additional intelligence you gather from additional technical signals is of great value.

Chart courtesy of StockCharts.com

Figure 6-11 Falling wedge pattern

This combined application of candlesticks and other indicators helps create a powerful system for entry and exit setup signals. The next chapter explores this topic further.

chapter 7

Buy and Sell Setup Signals

A long-term investor is likely to find candlestick patterns interesting, but will not use them to time short-term trades. In comparison, a trader who relies on candlesticks to time entry and exit decisions is going to rely on candlesticks (as well as traditional technical analysis and volume indicators) to *swing trade* in stock. The swing trader is anyone who wants to make moves in and out of positions to take short-term profits resulting from price spikes (in both directions) and the tendency of the market as a whole to overreact to news.

📖 Swing Trade

A trade with a short time in a position, entered after price spikes or percentages above the norm of movement; the purpose is to time short-term profits by trading contrary to the market tendency.

The swing trader rightly observes that the market exaggerates the importance of all news. This includes company-specific economic news, domestic and international economic developments, and political change. In other words, everything affects markets, but traders drive prices too high following good news and too low following bad news. The natural "swing" in price occurs when the overreaction creates buy and sell opportunities and reverses the direction. This situation normally occurs within two to five trading sessions after the spike.

> ✓ **Key Point**
> The key to short-term swing profits is recognizing overreaction in price to both good and bad news.

Traders rely on moving averages for the same reason. Short-term price movement is very chaotic and the result of an unknown number of cause-and-effect drivers. Whenever a dominant factor creates a large price swing, the swing trader makes a move, buying on price declines and selling (either selling an existing position or selling short) after prices have risen. Everyone has seen examples of this price tendency. For example, analysts have estimated that a company will report quarter earnings of 17 cents per share, but actual results come in at 16 cents. The stock loses four points on the day of the announcement but recovers three points over the following two days. This type of price overreaction is common. It dispels the efficient market hypothesis convincingly. An "efficient" market would react logically and reflect little if any movement on a specific day.

Instead, the tendency with bad news is to experience a two- to five-day set of gyrations in either direction or in both directions in turn. The net effect of news is realized over the entire swing. So a one-cent disappointment in earnings might justify a one-point drop, while actual price movement consists of a jarring four-point drop followed by a three-point reversal.

Rather than an efficient market, the short-term chaos in price reaction demonstrates that the market is driven by two primary emotions. When good news arrives, *greed* takes effect and drives prices up beyond a rational level. When bad news is announced, *fear* dominates and drives prices down too far. Swing traders are able to stand back from these short-term overreactions and recognize that they are extreme. So as *contrarian investors*, swing traders buy on price declines (knowing that prices are likely to recover) and sell on price increases (knowing that prices are likely to retreat).

> 📖 **Contrarian Investor**
> A trader or investor who recognizes that markets overreact to news and who makes buy and sell decisions in a direction opposite the prevailing trend.

> ✓ **Key Point**
> Two ruling emotions—greed and fear—cause virtually all the short-term price movement in the market, followed immediately by opposite correcting price changes. Knowing this is the key to finding entry and exit points.

Price Spikes and Reaction Swings

The well-known price spikes that are typical of price movement, notably in volatile markets, create reaction swings, providing swing traders with a great opportunity. At these times, candlestick signs, moves, and patterns are valuable in improving timing and confirming the best timing of entry into and exit from positions.

A price *spike* is any change in price above or below the established trading range. Although a spike may signal the beginning of a new trend, it more often is followed by a return to the previous range. This realization points out the advantage to using spikes as setup signals for short-term profits.

Spike

A sudden price move above or below the trading range, which often is followed by a return to that range within a few trading sessions.

When the spike is also accompanied by large increases in volume, it may signal a change in trading range. However, you will discover many spikes without any noticeable change in the typical level of trading. When volume does not spike along with price, this usually means that the spike has no lasting importance. In fact, it often occurs that prices spike with no change in volume *until* the price returns to previous levels. When this situation occurs—price spike with no change in volume, followed by a return to previous volume levels and a price spike—it normally signals that the price is not moving to a new range. Swing traders can take advantage of these short-term adjustments and overreactions by viewing the false-signal spike as an entry signal. On the downside, it works as a buy signal (or a signal to close out a previously opened short position), and on the upside, it serves as a signal to sell short (or to close previously opened long positions).

Some examples make this point. First is the quarterly chart of Procter & Gamble (PG). This chart, shown in Figure 7-1, contains an unusual spike that does not appear as a price move in a single day, but rather as a long lower shadow. However, this downward spike does not sustain a downward price movement.

Figure 7-1 Nonrecurring price spike

In this case, the lower shadow fell extremely far below the range, but the fact that the day's closing price was within the range reveals that the spike was not a trading range adjustment. Second, because volume did not spike at the same time as the price spike, the aberration of the long lower shadow could have signaled a swing trader to enter the position at the bottom of the spike or to close short positions when that occurred. The key here was the lack of change in volume as the spike was taking place.

> ✓ **Key Point**
>
> *A price spike is most significant when volume also moves upward. When there is no big change in volume, the spike is probably going to retreat immediately.*

A completely different situation evolved in the case of Intel Corporation (INTC). This chart, shown in Figure 7-2, reveals a very large price gap at the spike *and* significant increase in volume. For swing traders, this signals a complete breakout away from the existing trading range.

7 Buy and Sell Setup Signals

Figure 7-2 Spike with breakaway and new range

The pattern is clear. The spike is accompanied by a price gap and exceptionally high volume. Immediately after this strong move, a new support and resistance range are created and sustained.

Candlesticks also play an important role in this kind of move. Note how the clear downtrend is followed by an equally clear uptrend right before the spike. This trend conforms to the widely accepted point concerning candlestick patterns. As long as the uptrend continues, swing traders should remain long in this position. It was not until the first week of August that a three-day downward pattern emerged. However, the narrow-range day (NRD) and high volume in the last week of July served as a clear sign that the strong uptrend was ending.

If the spike is more typical of a short-term price adjustment, you expect to see a retreat, as in the case of the intra-day action in Procter & Gamble (PG) shown in Figure 7-1. The return up to the previously established price range is called a *reaction swing*. Prices move in one direction in an exaggerated response to news and then react by moving back to previously established levels.

📖 Reaction Swing

A tendency for short-term prices to return to an established trading range following a price spike.

The reaction swing is easily recognized when it takes place in an isolated trading day; however, it also can occur within a single trading session, as in the case of the PG chart. However, caution is required in the sessions following a price spike. In the PG chart, a three-day uptrend followed shortly after prices returned to their normal range, and then a long black day. This scenario could be interpreted as a signal of a coming downtrend; however, remembering that the downward spike of the earlier session occurred, it pays to wait. The spike can be thought of as an attempt by sellers to drive prices down, but it did not succeed. At this point, it was much more likely that prices would rise than that they would fall. So the long black day is not a reliable signal in these conditions.

> ✓ **Key Point**
> *Recognizing the uncertainty of what will happen next is just as valuable as a clear reversal signal. Uncertainty is an indication to stay out of positions until the picture clears up.*

The uncertainty of price action during and after a price spike can lead to false signals, a time when additional confirmation such as volume trends are valuable. Another useful indicator is the occurrence of a new high or new low in prices on a 52-week basis. A spike may occur at such a time. If price has been trending downward and concludes with a downside spike at the 52-week low, that may be a strong signal that the downtrend is ending. If this confirms what you see in the candlestick pattern and volume of the same time, it works as a very good entry indicator. The same is true on the upside. As a stock's price reaches its 52-week high, experiences an upside spike, and also has exceptionally high volume, it works as a short-side entry signal or as a sell signal for previously entered long positions.

Percentage Swing Systems

Adhering to a candlestick-based system accompanied by volume and other indicators is perhaps the most reliable method of timing entry and exit from positions. An alternative is to rely on *percentage swing systems*, or systems signaling entry or exit based on the degree of price movement away from the previous trading range.

📖 Percentage Swing System

A method of timing entry and exit based on the percentage by which price moves above or below the previously establishing trading range.

The problem with the percentage system is that it is fixed and is not based on the patterns of candlesticks. The relative strength or weakness of an evolving candlestick price trend may not be supported in an inflexible percentage of change; it is more likely that strength or weakness in price movement is going to be reflected in candlestick patterns, even when only a small percentage of change has occurred. The percentage system works in varying degrees, occasionally giving out an entry or exit signal at the wrong time. For example in the six-month chart of Apple (AAPL), shown in Figure 7-3, a combination of signals was at work in July. Most important was a strong uptrend with price gaps. A percentage system could also be used, identifying a 10 percent increase in price over previous levels by the beginning of August.

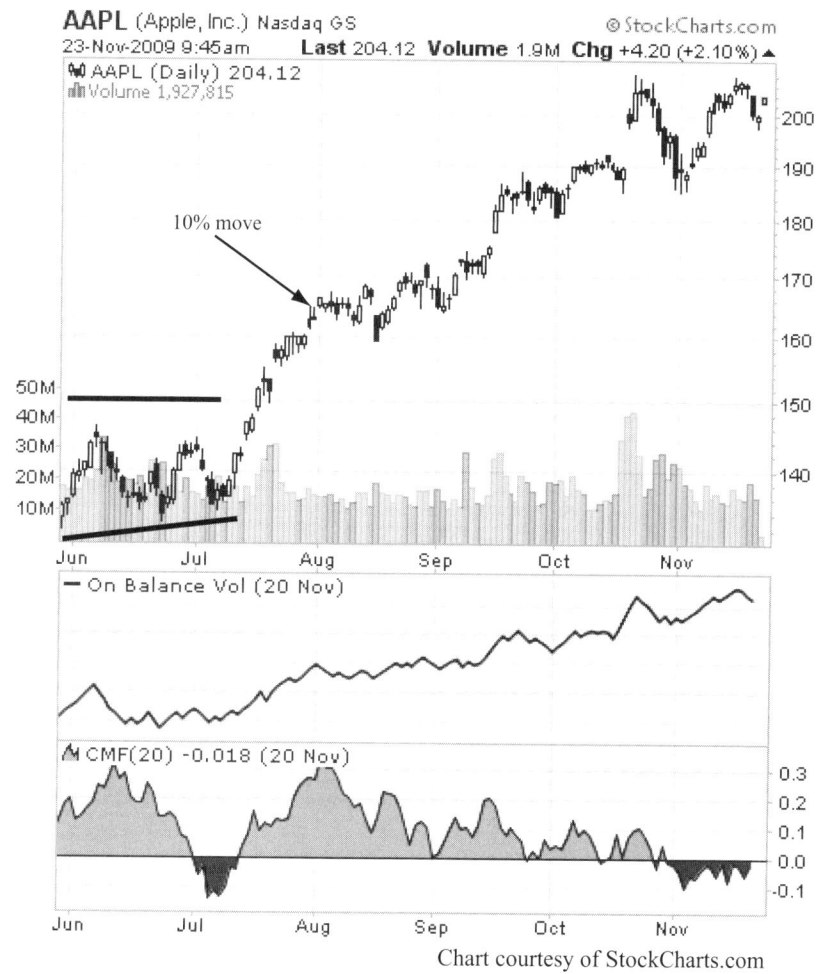

Chart courtesy of StockCharts.com

Figure 7-3 Percentage of change system—10 percent move

However, one of the problems with percentage-based systems is that signals often are recognized too late. If you waited for the 10 percent increase in price, you would enter this position *after* growth. A contrarian point of view after this growth would be to sell rather than to buy. Both decisions—buying after the uptrend or selling—would have been wrong in this case. A stronger signal to confirm a bullish stand is the combination of the candlestick formation with gaps and exceptionally high volume. Also note the bullish indicator below the chart in the CMF, which was very strong both in mid-June and early August.

> ✓ **Key Point**
>
> *Entry and exit based on percentage systems work at times, but not consistently. No matter how promising the approach sounds, your timing is going to be better if you focus on candlestick trends and not on price movement percentages.*

Another example of the percentage system was found in the six-month chart of Hewlett-Packard (HPQ). This one is shown in Figure 7-4.

In this situation, a much stronger and longer-lasting uptrend is revealed. It was first anticipated in three indicators. First was a very strong candlestick pattern with a gap and then breakout above resistance. Second was the 10 percent move in price. Third was the unusually high CMF indicator, which reached nearly 0.6. (An indicator passing 0.25 is considered strongly bullish.) In combination, these indicators all confirm the emerging uptrend that developed and lasted through the end of November, or a total of over four months. It is further interesting that at the conclusion of the chart, the CMF again emerged with a strongly bullish signal just below 0.25.

A percentage change system can be used as a confirming signal to candlestick patterns (further confirmed by additional technical indicators such as CMF or on-balance volume). It can also be applied in a contrarian manner. For example, if price moves up 10 percent, that is seen as a sign of a coming correction. In both of the examples provided, that would not have worked. The uptrend in both Apple and Hewlett-Packard continued well after the 10 percent move.

Figure 7-4 Percentage of change system—clear uptrend

Short-Term Gapping Behavior

A more reliable timing system than percentage change is based on tracking a stock's "true range," or the analysis of price movement between days rather than in an isolated single-day range. In the typical daily trading range, the previous day's activity is completely ignored. This is the most popular method, but it ignores what often is extremely valuable information.

📖 True Range

A stock's trading range within a trend rather than a single trading session. It includes the previous session's closing price and the current session's price movement.

✓ Key Point

The trend looks amazingly different when changes between days are taken into account. The true range clarifies the trend and points out the flaw in myopic review only of session-specific action.

True range consists of the previous session's closing price, carried through to the current session's price movement. In this analysis, you seek the otherwise invisible gaps that often take place between days. The obvious gaps are easy to spot. The range of a candlestick's trades gaps from day to day. But another type of gap may be equally significant. It is the overnight change between prior close and current open. This *gapping trend* can occur in a number of configurations, which are summarized in Figure 7-5.

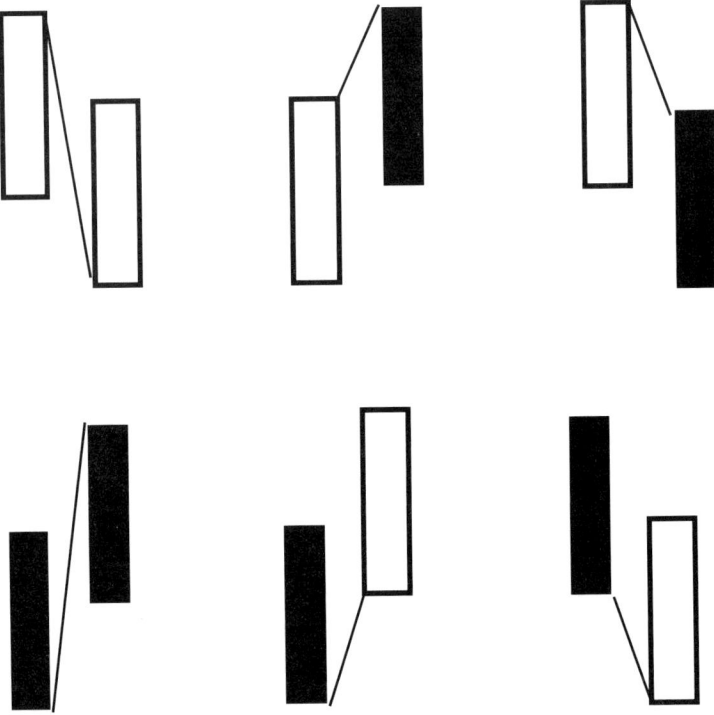

Figure 7-5   Overnight gapping trends

📖 Gapping Trend

Any trend involving price gaps, especially between trading sessions in which the gaps are not immediately visible.

It is important to recognize that the real bodies in all six of these moves overlap between days. This means that the overnight gapping trend is invisible. If you look only at each day's open and close, you will not notice this important gapping trend. There are six instances shown in which the intra-day gapping trend occurs. The most severe involve two consecutive white or black candlesticks in which the current white session has a lower real body range than the previous day, or when the current black candlestick's range is higher. However, even in those sessions with less extreme gaps, the occurrence of gapping trends (especially when they occur in a repetitive series) is very significant.

Two quarterly charts demonstrate how this invisible gapping trend affects chart interpretation. The first is the chart of Yahoo! (YHOO), shown in Figure 7-6.

Chart courtesy of StockCharts.com

Figure 7-6 Gapping trend anticipating bearish price movement

There are five important gaps on this chart. The first one is visible and anticipates a price reversal. The second, however, is invisible, and although the intraday gap is small, it was also the signal of the start of a strong uptrend. The third gap was very similar to the second. The fourth spanned one-half of a point and signaled a coming downtrend. The most important of all the gaps was the fifth and largest. The visible gap between the two days was only one-quarter of a point, but the true range gap of the two-day price change was over two points, from the first day's close at approximately 17.25 down to the close of the second day at about 15.10. The range of this downward movement is not visible if you look only at the space between candles from one day to the next.

> ✓ **Key Point**
>
> *A visible gap is easy to spot, but it is not always the entire picture. Remember to study gaps with the true distance between open and close between the days involved to judge the gap's real extent.*

Another example of the gapping trend is seen in the quarterly chart for McDonald's (MCD). This one is shown in Figure 7-7.

Chart courtesy of StockCharts.com

Figure 7-7 Gapping trend in recurring pattern

This chart is interesting because it displays a series of repetitive gaps during an uptrend, followed by a strong and very sudden reversal. As a general observation, when you see a series of gaps, it is likely that the price is moving too far in one direction; a reversal should be expected. This trend occurs on the upside with three consecutive days of price gaps between sessions. Then the big decline hits and the visible portion of the gap is easy to spot. However, the intraday gap of the two sessions is more extreme, consisting of the high close of the white candlestick down to the low close of the black candlestick on the following day. An astute chartist would have known that the three consecutive upward price gaps represented a danger signal. When the final white candle in the uptrend displayed a very long upper shadow but a fairly small real body, it signaled the end of the uptrend (especially following on the unusual three-day gapping pattern).

Anticipating the Trend During Consolidation

Entry and exit setup signals help you anticipate coming price direction, whether reversal or continuation. A swing trading strategy that you, as an individual, employ is especially effective when playing with price movement caused by the institutional investor. Your advantage consists of two facts. First, the majority of price movement and its cause and effect belong to the institutional investors. Second, you can move quickly in and out of positions without having to worry that a big block trade will influence the price. Institutional investors have to act slowly and cautiously because of their influence on stock prices.

This reality points to a clear advantage you hold over institutions. You are able to move in and out of positions by trading on the emotions that rule the market. Most trades take place based on reaction to institutional influence. This is why greed (on the way up) and fear (on the way down) are the driving forces behind the majority of individual stock trades. If you are able to put aside the normal tendency to trade based on these emotions, you stand an excellent chance of improving your entry and exit timing.

> ✓ **Key Point**
>
> *Individuals can move quickly and easily in and out of positions. This is an advantage over the large institutional investor who cannot move large blocks as readily.*

Swing trading is a system based on exploiting the very short-term price trends resulting from the emotions that dominate the market. Traders who adhere to this system focus on a short list of stocks with the desirable attributes: moderate volatility, strong technical signals, and a tendency to track the market closely. (Thus, when the indicators rise, so does the stock, and vice versa.) A swing trader working with a short list of favored stocks trades the emotions of the market in a two- to five-day range, rather than trading the stocks based on fundamental merit. A swing trader may initially select stocks based on the strength of fundamentals as part of the selection criteria, but timing entry and exit requires recognition of candlestick patterns, unusual volume spikes, changes in volatility, and proven technical indicators like CMF.

When you trade emotions instead of stocks, your entry and exit timing is likely to improve vastly because you acknowledge the overreaction of price based on the greed and fear that are present at all times in the market. The only respite comes during periods of sideways price movement, and that rarely lasts long. Swing traders, in fact, rely on an uninformed and overreacting marketplace to recognize opportunities. As a swing trader, you interact with market forces by knowing when other traders are ready to give up shares of stock too cheaply, or buy shares from you that have become too expensive. Making decisions based on rational, calculated observation does not come naturally to most people. Most people do time their moves emotionally, and this is a great advantage to the analytical swing trader.

The pauses between uptrends and downtrends—periods of *consolidation*—occur because buyers and sellers are more or less in agreement about two points. First, the relatively narrow trading range appears to be reasonable for the moment. Second, no one knows which trend will take place next. The emotion that dominates this sideways price period of consolidation is uncertainty. Few people are content with knowing that buyers and sellers agree on price. It is preferable to recognize when one side or the other is in command.

📖 Consolidation

A period in which a narrow trading range is in effect and little if any movement occurs. It is likely to occur in between upward or downward trends and reflects uncertainty in the market about future price direction.

In some periods of consolidation, it is not uncertainty but confusion that rules price. It may also mean that most technical traders do not know how to read the trend, so both buyers and sellers wait out the market. This is where reading candlestick moves and patterns can help you get a jump on the next trend. Two examples demonstrate how this works. First is the quarterly chart of American Express (AXP), shown in Figure 7-8.

In this chart, a one-month period of consolidation suddenly breaks out to the upside. This was not impossible to predict; in fact, chartists should have noticed the two white marubozu candles one week apart. These patterns showed that buyers were about to take control of the trend.

✓ Key Point

Some candlesticks—even single-day ones—anticipate a trend that might occur several sessions later. The cause and effect are not always instantaneous.

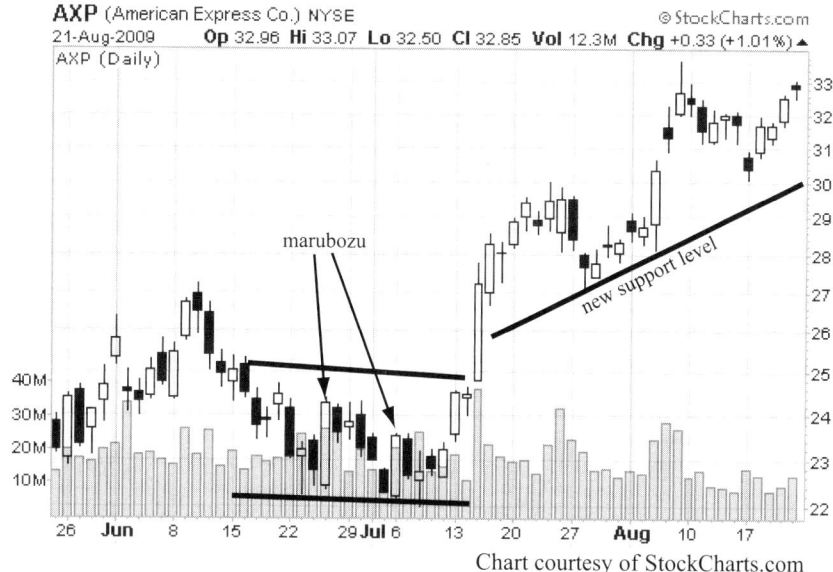

Figure 7-8 Consolidation with marubozu breakout

In another chart, this one for Bank of America (BAC) shown in Figure 7-9, a different candlestick pattern predicted that consolidation was about to end.

Figure 7-9 Consolidation with inverse head and shoulders

This example marks the period of consolidation, which concludes with a short-term downtrend that concluded with a clear inverse head-and-shoulders pattern. The price began moving upward but did not break off the consolidation range until a third short-term downtrend was set (at the second shoulder). This was a strong confirming indicator of a coming uptrend, and an inverse head and shoulders.

The Setup Pattern and Swing

Every trader seeks a reliable set of indicators to improve timing of both entry and exit. In this quest, there is a tendency to emphasize entry signals but to overlook the equally important exit. Because swing trading involves moving into long positions at the bottom of the swing and into short positions at the top, many entry signals for one side double as exit signals for the other. For example, if you recognize a reversal signal at the top of the trend, you immediately close out your long position. Do you open a short position in the same stock at the same time? This is the decision every short-term trader has to make.

In a sense, replacing a long with a short or a short with a long doubles your risk exposure. Taking a short-term profit on one trend does not guarantee that you will repeat the experience as price is expected to move in the opposite direction. However, a true swing trader will want to maximize the advantage of playing both sides of the swing. Doing so requires skill in pattern recognition. The stronger the reversal signal, the better your timing will become. Swing traders have to be concerned with two issues. First, they want to get the most from the swing trade, which means knowing when an apparent signal is false and no action should be taken. Second is to know when to close the current position and whether to wait out the trend or perform a true swing.

You can use candlestick moves and patterns not only to identify a short-term trend but also to decide how strong or weak the signal is. Some signals are quite strong and are confirmed by candlestick developments, volume changes, and other technical patterns. Others are tentative or contradictory. Identifying the difference further improves your timing in entering and exiting the swing trade.

There is a point in every trend in which the "last gasp" of price movement is apparent. This point is easily recognized in hindsight when you look back to see what signals were there just before the price turned. It is not as easy to spot these signs at the time. The key is to seek combinations of signals that confirm one another. However, it is also crucial to realize that some signals provide false indicators.

> ✓ **Key Point**
>
> Confirmation is the key to chart analysis and timing of both entry and exit. Candlestick patterns combined with other technical indicators improve your interpretation of trends.

Three important combinations of signals follow with examples of both true and false instances of each.

Marubozu with Volume Spike

The first double-indicator sign of a price turn is the combined appearance of the marubozu (long candle with little or no upper or lower shadow) along with a spike in volume. This is one of the strongest signs of a reversal when the marubozu is black after an uptrend, or white at the end of a downtrend. If the opposite conditions are found (black marubozu after a downtrend or white after an uptrend), this combined indicator can also work as a continuation pattern.

An example of this double indicator was seen in the six-month chart of Alcoa (AA), shown in Figure 7-10.

This combined indicator signals the end of the uptrend very strongly. The very fast uptrend preceding the marubozu included four price gaps in four days, a further indication that the price level was due for a correction. It is noteworthy that at the bottom of the ensuing downtrend, a second marubozu appeared. However, there was no price-based confirmation that the downtrend was going to continue. In fact, the downtrend (like the uptrend preceding) was quite fast. The CMF indicator could have been viewed as confirming the bearish sign at the bottom of the downtrend, but as subsequent price movement revealed, this was a false indicator. A more disturbing false marubozu with volume spike was found in the six-month chart of Best Buy (BBY), which is shown in Figure 7-11.

Chart courtesy of StockCharts.com

Figure 7-10 Marubozu with volume spike

Figure 7-11 False indicator: marubozu with volume spike

✓ Key Point

A marubozu is one of the strongest single-stick signals. When you see this sign, pay attention.

This example includes a marubozu that did not strictly conform to the required attributes. It was closer to a long black candle because the session did include some upper and lower shadows. The spike in volume is also disturbing because prices did not fall as you might expect in these conditions. In fact, this occurred during a period of gradually increasing price levels. The mixed signals seen on this chart should lead you to close out positions and wait out clearer signals or focus on different stocks.

Price Gap with Volume Spike

The second form of confirming signals involves the combination of a clear price gap with spikes in volume. This signal is often seen as the kick-off for a strong trend in either direction, but as with all signals, the combination can also provide a false lead.

A good example of this trend was found in the six-month chart of Caterpillar (CAT), shown in Figure 7-12.

Figure 7-12   Price gap with volume spike

The uptrend immediately before this was quite strong and contained three gapping days, moving price seven points in only six sessions. The occurrence of the large price gap with the volume spike is a continuation indicator. This is further confirmed by the dramatic change in the CMF, moving during the same period from minus 0.2 to positive 0.2, and then even further to a very bullish level above 0.3. However, as strong as this particular pattern was, it is also possible for the price gap with volume spike to put out a false signal. For example, Kraft Foods (KFT) displayed a large downward price gap with a volume spike. Based on the bullish pattern displayed by Caterpillar (Figure 7-12), you would assume that the bearish indicator in the case of Kraft, shown in Figure 7-13, would predict a strong downturn.

Chart courtesy of StockCharts.com

Figure 7-13 False indicator: price gap with volume spike

> ✓ **Key Point**
>
> *A simple observation of changes in price and volume together is one form of confirming technical information that usually points out exactly which direction price is heading next.*

This pattern looks bearish and is confirmed further by on-balance volume and CMF trends. However, as the subsequent chart reveals, price support is strong after the strong downward gap and volume spike. This pattern demonstrates that the combined indicators, while strong, are not always reliable. In fact, this gapping trend is a correction of price levels that rose too far, too fast. In hindsight, this is easily spotted. However, in the moment, it is not as obvious. For this reason, it is productive to review emerging patterns in a context not only of what is taking place now, but in the past as well.

CMF Move with Repetitive Price Gaps

The third combined indicator includes price gaps and CMF trends. This one, like the previous combined indicators, can easily prove to be a false signal. In swing trading, there are no certainties. However, the point of tracking candlestick charts with other confirming indicators is to improve your chances of being right more often. Entry and exit timing is the key to generating the short-term profits you seek from swing trading.

An example of the combined CMF and repetitive price gap signal was found in the six-month chart of Boeing (BA), shown in Figure 7-14.

There are multiple bullish signals during this strong uptrend. The price gaps are the most important in the series of white candlesticks. The uptrend overreaches, retreats, and then moves once again. However, note the difference in the various uptrends in the CMF line. In the first, in which the price gaps are present, CMF has moved strongly upward above 0.25. The second uptrend is accompanied by the CMF remaining at a high level. However, the third uptrend is contradicted by a declining CMF. The lack of confirmation during this third move should prevent against entering a long position.

7 Buy and Sell Setup Signals

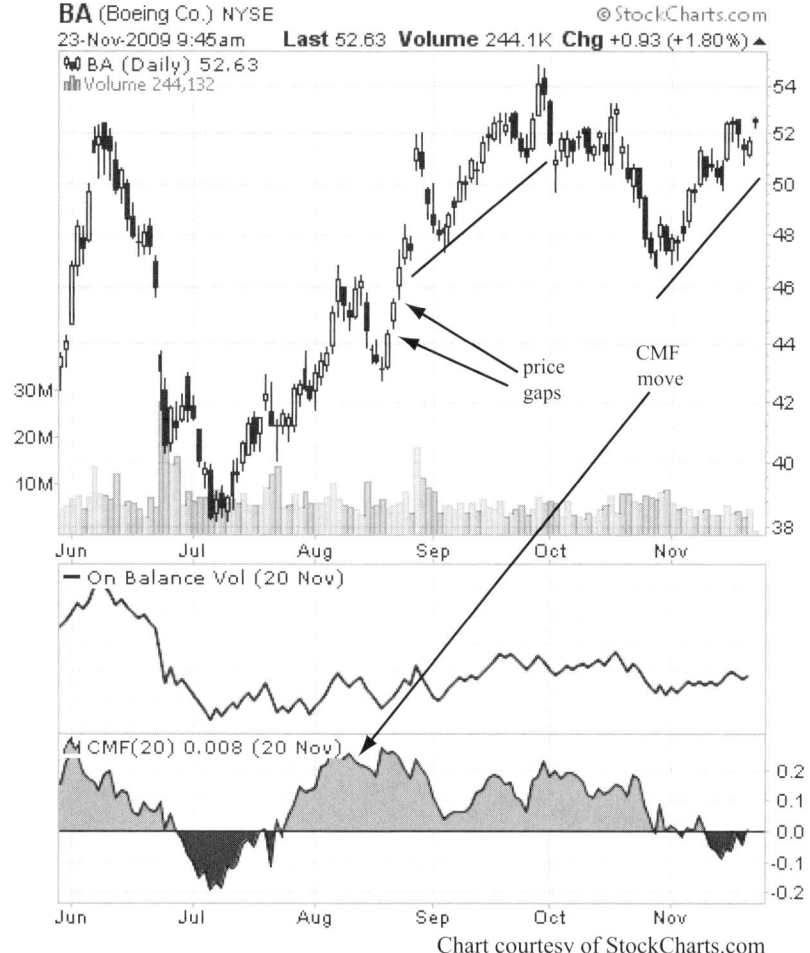

Chart courtesy of StockCharts.com

Figure 7-14 CMF move with repetitive price gaps

✓ Key Point

Price gaps are very important indicators, and so is the CMF trend. In combination, however, they provide a strong signal of impending price direction.

The combination of CMF and repetitive price gaps can also represent a false signal. For example, the six-month chart for Chevron (CVX) contains a false signal, which is shown in Figure 7-15.

Figure 7-15   False indicator: CMF move with repetitive price gaps

The strong downtrend with multiple price gaps appears very bearish. Accompanying this was the negative trend in CMF, which fell below −0.2. However, the trend that followed was strongly bullish. The CMF acknowledged this by moving up above 0.4, which was exceptionally strong. However, the initial indication that prices would continue downward did not come to pass. Even before the strong bullish move in CMF, the candlestick formation turned very bullish immediately and established an uptrend that contradicted the combined downward CMF and repetitive price gaps.

Support and Resistance in the Swing Trade

The confirmation of signals in the isolation of a few trading sessions can be revealing, but it always makes more sense to look at the emerging pattern in a larger context. How does the apparent signal conform with (or contradict) established support and resistance levels?

As a general observation, trading remains within the established trading range. When a breakout occurs, prices will quickly retreat in many instances as a trend is reversed. The exception is a breakout that remains permanent. The new range will be tested, and a tendency is for one side or the other to overextend, requiring a range correction immediately afterward. This general rule of thumb helps to further determine whether a signal or combination of signals is exceptionally strong or suspiciously weak.

✓ Key Point

Most short-term traders take comfort in prices remaining in the trading range. Breakouts are exciting and unavoidable, but they introduce more risk and more uncertainty as well.

The trading range, bordered by resistance at the top and support at the bottom, is the visual summary of supply and demand for a company's shares. Swing traders generally operate within the trading range, with prices bouncing between resistance and support and presenting short-term profit opportunities. A conservative-leaning swing trader may close out positions when prices go through a breakout, recognizing that any number of scenarios can play out. For the "range-bound" swing trader, this is a safe hedge against the possibility of making an expensive mistake by misreading the signals. What may work reliably within an established trading range could present falsely during and after a breakout period. This is especially true for the confirming technical signals presented together in the previous section: marubozu candles, volume spikes, gaps, and CMF moves. They all are strong signals within a trading range and may even predict breakouts. But after a breakout has taken place (as many of the previously presented charts display), false signals are more likely.

Combining candlestick moves and patterns with the position in a trading range (or, more to the point, when prices go through a breakout), you will be able to judge buy and sell set-up signals more accurately. In studying candlestick patterns in both cases—those resulting in breakout and those with price remaining range-bound—you can judge the strength of support and resistance and better determine the significance of a trend.

Examples follow, all based on quarterly charts showing only price and volume. The first two involve situations in which price broke out of the established range; the third and fourth demonstrate why trend signals remained within the trading range. First is the case of Pfizer (PFE), which is shown in Figure 7-16.

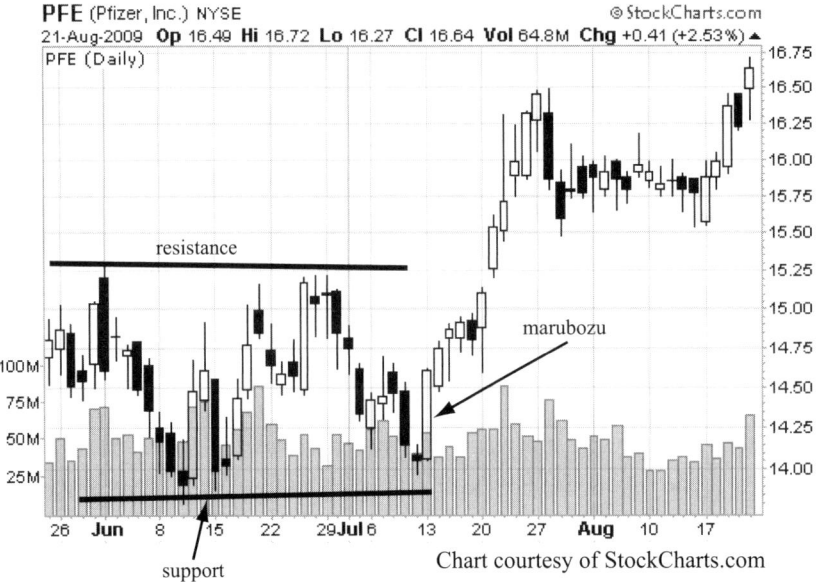

Figure 7-16 Price breakout following marubozu

The white marubozu pointed out on this chart is the signal of the coming upside breakout. Also note the long white candle day 11 sessions earlier. It preceded a downtrend that ended with the white marubozu, presenting a very strong reversal signal. The subsequent uptrend set a new support level about two points above the previous one. This is a typical instance in which the breakout was signaled ahead of time. The classic double top seen in the established trading range was offset by a double bottom, so this classic technical sign was a wash. Both upside and downside moves were implied, but the marubozu was a far stronger signal.

> ✓ **Key Point**
>
> *Some technical signals contradict one another as price bounces back and forth within the trading range. At such times, seek a strong candlestick-based development to anticipate a price breakout.*

Another breakout was signaled by another candlestick. Unlike the single-stick sign in the form of a marubozu, this was anticipated by a two-session move, the bullish harami. It shows up at the bottom of a downtrend in the chart of Wal-Mart (WMT), as shown in Figure 7-17.

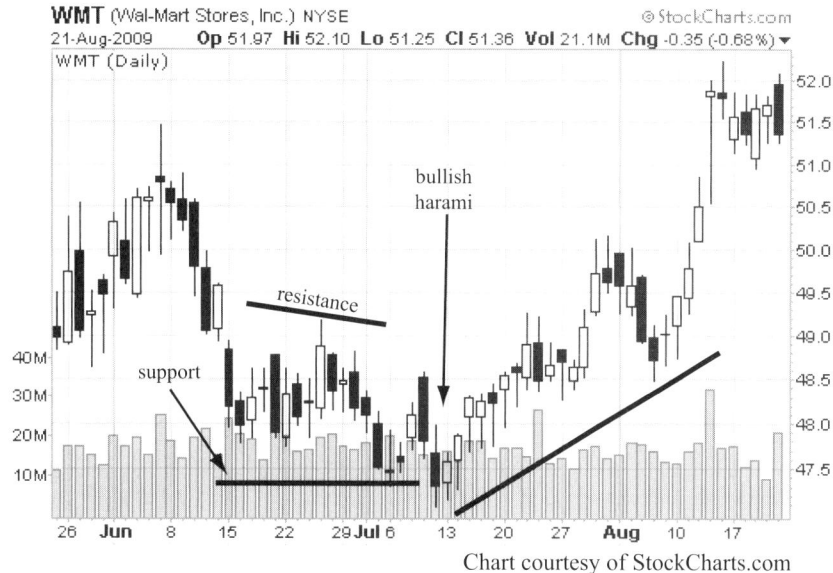

Chart courtesy of StockCharts.com

Figure 7-17 **Price breakout following bullish harami**

This move showed up after two black candlestick sessions. If a third black session had shown up, it would have signaled a downtrend, especially because it would have broken down through support. However, the appearance of the harami is a very strong bullish signal that accurately predicted the end of the current trading range and a move higher.

> ✓ **Key Point**
>
> *The harami is a subtle, often unimpressive-looking move. But it often signals a big reversal.*

Some patterns remain in the existing range, and indicators reveal that a breakout is unlikely. For swing trading purposes, it is desirable to be able to rely on an established range and predictable short-term uptrends and downtrends in repetitive patterns. For example, the chart for Coca-Cola (KO) demonstrably set up short-term price movement without any expectation of a breakout in the near future. This example is shown in Figure 7-18.

Figure 7-18 Trend with marubozu but no breakout

The current trading range was set up with an exceptionally strong white marubozu at the end of May. Resistance stays within a half-point range of 50 to 50.50 for the remainder of the chart, with the exception of a failed upside breakout attempt. As it often occurs, the rise in price was quite fast at the point of breakout, and the retreat back into range was very fast as well. Support also remained in a half-point range between 47 and 47.50. The most important aspect of this sequence of short-term trends is that even with very strong signals in the form of long white candles, uptrends with gaps, and two marubozu days, the range held.

Another example of a short-term trend without breakout was seen in the chart of Microsoft (MSFT), which is summarized in Figure 7-19.

This example shows an easily spotted failed attempt at breakout. The very strong and fast uptrend moving above resistance and including gapping action on the way up is obvious. However, the price immediately retreats back into range with a very significant gap, a sign that the attempt could not sustain a new level. The existing range held strongly for the rest of the chart. The upside gap was a troubling one as well because no clear uptrend was established before the attempted breakout. An uptrend requires at least three upward sessions. The pattern here was two upward sessions followed by small black candlestick, and then the gap and a repeat of the pattern. In other words, even though price was moving upward, it lacked the strength you would expect to see in a true breakout.

Figure 7-19 Trend with gaps but no breakout

The entire analysis of candlestick patterns makes sense when combined with other technical indicators and, equally important, when reviewed in the context of basics such as the trading range and the existence of double or triple tops and bottoms, head-and-shoulders formations, and other well-known technical chart developments. In the next chapter, the discussion of how to use technical indicators is expanded to explain how to effectively improve swing trading techniques.

chapter 8

Swing Trading with Candlesticks

The preceding chapter on finding buy and sell setup signals made the point that some very distinct patterns emerge to help you improve your timing. This approach—short-term trading based on the tendency of markets to overreact to both good and bad news—is widely known as *swing trading*. However, far from a "sure thing," even the strongest patterns and best forms of confirmation give out false signals at times. There are ways to recognize the subtle differences between a breakout or reversal, and the coincidental movement of prices and shapes of candlesticks. This chapter explores this issue further by describing some additional technical tools you can use to expand swing trading and the timing of entry and exit. This type of trading depends on the effective use of candlestick signs, moves, and patterns (those one-, two-, and three-day indicators that represent the essential insights from candlestick analysis).

A Swing Trading Overview

The "swing" involved with swing trading is usually described solely as movement of price between high and low levels. These levels are usually the trading range bordered by resistance and support. These swings usually take place between two and five days, although short-term trends can last longer as well. Entry and exit signals consist of popular patterns and developments, including the development of consecutive up and down candles. These signals are defined as a series of days with higher highs and higher lows (uptrend) or lower lows and lower highs (downtrend). The second popular swing trading signal is the narrow-range day (NRD), better known among candlestick chartists as a doji. The third of three strong signals is an unusually high-volume spike. Combinations of signals are exceptionally strong indicators of reversal. So when a short-term candlestick trend concludes with a doji, it is very possible that the price direction is about to change. The doji combined with a volume spike is even stronger. It means that all trading for the day took place within a very small range and that volume was nonetheless quite large.

> ✓ **Key Point**
> *Swing trading signals require confirmation before being acknowledged as definite entry or exit indicators. Confirmation is the key element to identifying an action point.*

Swing traders use these well-known indicators. Because trading is done on the swing, there are a few variations of the technique, and they are worth examining:

1. *Entry only at the bottom.* The most conservative swing trader wants to avoid shorting stock. This trader believes shorting to be far too risky to include in a strategy. As a result, only bottom-swing, long-side transactions are made. The trader looks for an entry signal at the bottom of a downtrend and an exit at the top.

    The advantage to bottom-only entry is that it restricts activity to long positions, making it a lower-risk approach. The disadvantage is that it misses half of the opportunities inherent in swing trading. The swing trader has to acknowledge that overreaction within the market takes place not only after a downtrend, but also after an uptrend. So in exchange for less risk, the long position swing trader takes part only in reversals of downtrends. In markets that are overbought and due for downside correction, there are going to be many missed opportunities.

2. *Entry only at the top.* An exceptionally bearish swing trader believes that the market is generally overbought and due for downside corrections. Accordingly, this trader views uptrends as aberrations in the longer-term bear market. Distrustful of any uptrend, the bear-oriented swing trader—like the bottom-only long trader—misses half of the swing trading opportunities. The top-only trader shorts stock when uptrends show signs of reversal or uses long puts to play the market in the same way but with less risk.

    The major advantage to this approach is that when the bear is correct, the short-term downtrends tend to be rapid and extreme. So a bear swing trader is likely to earn many short-term profits above those of the swing trader entering at the bottom for short-term uptrends. The big disadvantage is that the bear trader trusts only half of the swing opportunities and uses shorted stock in a higher-risk strategy, or uses long puts while not also using long calls at the bottom.

3. *Entry and exit at the same time on both sides.* The true swing trader is not concerned with long-term market trends but focuses on exploiting overreaction by other traders. This trader recognizes that short-term price movement is emotional and often irrational, and fast moves represent short-term opportunities on both sides of the trade. As a result, the true swing trader enters a long stock position at the bottom of a downtrend and exits at the top. Using the same point of view about uptrends, reversal signals lead to short entry at the top and closing of the position at the bottom. The dual approach can be employed on a single stock or on different stocks going through varying trends. For example, one issue may be bottoming out at the same time that another is going through a strong uptrend.

The advantage to swing trading on both sides is that it enables you to take part in market overreaction in both uptrends and downtrends. It can also be employed on a range of stocks at the same time, but undergoing a variety of different price trends. The disadvantage is that playing both sides of the swing doubles risk exposure. It also requires shorting at the top if stock positions are employed in the strategy instead of long puts.

The best-understood definition of swing trading involves entry and exit at both sides of the swing. The flexibility allows you to enter and exit positions based on current conditions. It can also apply to a single stock. In that case, a reversal signal involves two transactions: closing a current swing position in one direction and opening another at the same time. Thus, as an uptrend signals a reversal, a long position is closed and replaced with a short position; and as a downtrend concludes, the short is closed and replaced with an offsetting long position.

✓ Key Point

Many swing trade action points involve both exit and entry; however, this also doubles your risk. A poorly timed double move equals twice the potential loss.

This approach doubles the risk, of course. If the timing is wrong or the two-part transaction is made in response to a false signal, you not only lose the opportunity for further profits in the first position, but also stand to lose more in the replacement position. For this reason, it makes sense to isolate uptrends and downtrends between two or more different stocks. When a current trend ends, the position is exited. Re-entry does not occur in that issue until a new signal emerges. This course of action is more prudent than a close-and-open reverse swing position. However, depending on the strength of the reversal indicator, it is wise to keep an open mind about the strategic and risk approach and to apply a strategy that makes sense at the time. This approach requires astute analysis of confirmation signals as well as awareness of the entry and exit indicators in the context of the longer-term trading range and other technical signals.

For the candlestick chart analyst, the "swing" should involve much more than just the price trend. This concept may seem contrary to widely accepted definitions of swing trading, but realistically, you know that swings also occur in trading range, moving averages (MAs), and technical indicators. (CMF is one strong indicator of strength or weakness, for example.) Analysis of price in short-term trends is based on price with nonprice indicators (such as volume spikes). However, if you combine these well-established indicators with an in-depth analysis of candlestick signs, moves, and patterns, you soon realize that it is not just price movement but the strength or weakness of that movement that really defines entry and exit in a swing trade.

✓ Key Point
Spotting a dual entry/exit point requires confirmation from additional technical signals beyond candlestick patterns.

Quantifying Price Movement with Candlesticks

Candlesticks are not just part of a setup; they are visual summaries of entry and exit strength or weakness. You need the visual aid because it displays *all* of the attributes of a trend including its strength or weakness, in a single glance. Beyond the visible uptrend and downtrend so readily acknowledged as it occurs, the collective signals beyond price are visible together. When you look backward at a chart, you can see what occurred and it is obvious. However, in the moment, a trend is far less certain. For example, an uptrend involving 12 days of strong movement will end somewhere. However, after the third, fifth, or seventh day of the trend, how do you know when the move is weakening? Price movement can be quantified with observation of collective technical trends beyond price alone. The candlestick moves and patterns are the primary indicators, but at the time you are watching a trend develop, you need more information.

8 Swing Trading with Candlesticks

✓ Key Point

Treating candlestick patterns as primary indicators is a good starting point; however, you also need to rely on nonprice technical signs.

Two examples make the point that in addition to analysis of the candlesticks, other signals can and should be brought to the table. The overall analysis is vastly improved by their inclusion. First is the six-month chart of Yahoo! (YHOO), shown in Figure 8-1.

Chart courtesy of StockCharts.com

Figure 8-1 Multiple reversal signals: example 1

Yahoo! was very volatile during this six-month period, and although price covered only a four-point range, it moved considerably and with many specific reversal signals—both in candlesticks and in other indicators. These trend reversals included the following combinations of indicators:

1. A white marubozu in the second session followed immediately by an upside gap.
2. A brief uptrend topped off with an isolated black spinning top. Because this trend appeared midway during a brief period of consolidation, it signaled a coming reversal of the previous uptrend.
3. A black marubozu at the end of the downtrend, followed by a second spinning top and then immediately by a strong white candle confirming the end of the downtrend and signaling the start of a reversal uptrend.
4. A gap in the uptrend followed by another brief consolidation. The gap was an indication that in this uptrend the price moved upward too quickly and was due for a reversal. Note how, as the trend began to reverse, the gap was filled with a downward-moving gap.
5. A long black candle after the downside gap, accompanied by very high volume. At the same time, the CMF fell rapidly and moved into negative territory.
6. An uptrend with strong gapping action. However, instead of the price moving too rapidly and due for a correction, note that CMF moved upward at the same time, supporting the indication of a continuation in the uptrend. This uptrend did not peak until the three days of high volume. When this volume signal occurred without a corresponding continuation in the trend, it indicated a coming reversal. As the pattern consolidated, note how CMF moved rapidly downward before the price trend turned.
7. The downtrend occurred as expected in the chart's last major trend movement. Note the long black candle signaling that the downtrend was not over, even after the preceding spinning top candle. There was at least one additional point of price drop yet to come, which was further confirmed by CMF remaining in the negative.

This chart provides numerous clues about reversal with confirming signals. Even with its relatively small point range, it was an ideal candidate for swing trading because price revealed a lot of in-range movement. You may see a similar well-defined range of movement in stocks with a larger range, but the same tendency to remain between resistance and support. An example was seen in Exxon-Mobil over a six-month period, as shown in Figure 8-2.

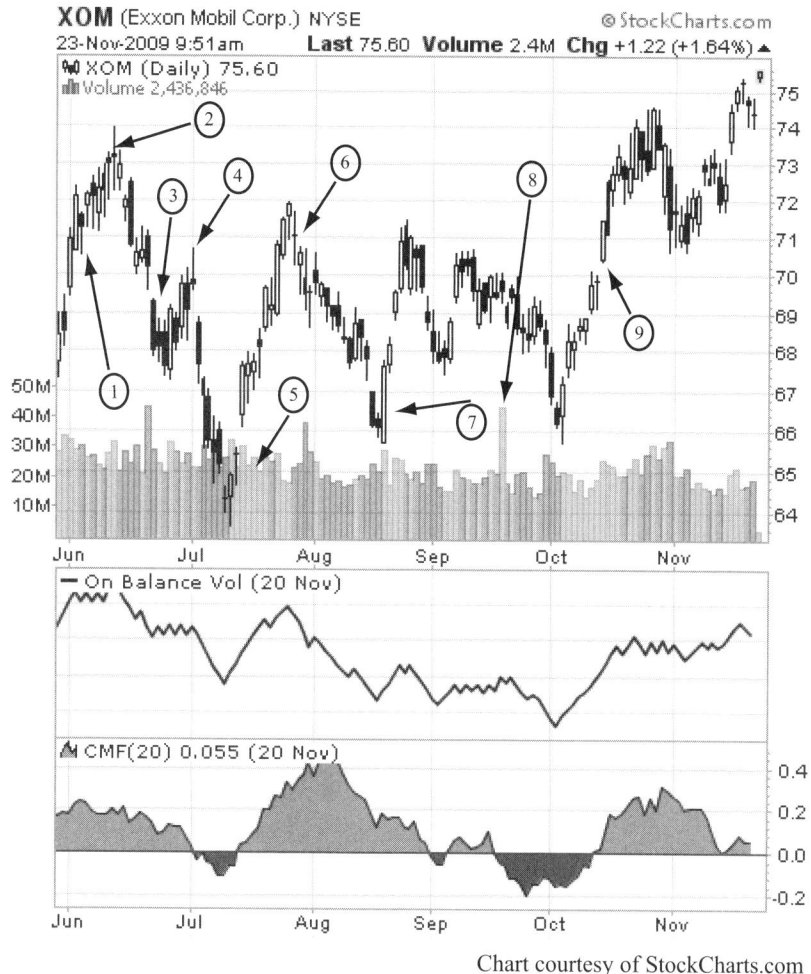

Chart courtesy of StockCharts.com

Figure 8-2 Multiple reversal signals: example 2

The number of confirming signals in this example are just as plentiful as in the previous one, but in a 120-point trading range instead of only 4 points. These signals include

1. Two long white candles taking place one after the other, an unusual sequence anticipating a continuation of upward movement.
2. A spinning top and falling CMF, signaling the top of the uptrend and reversal.
3. A long black candle with exceptionally high volume.
4. A spinning top with declining CMF and on-balance volume.

5. Two spinning tops occurring within three sessions, an unusual pattern that signals the end of the downtrend.
6. A spinning top after a rapid rise in prices, accurately anticipating a price retreat.
7. A long white candle followed by a gapping pattern; as soon as this uptrend stopped and revealed a black candle, this became a reversal point.
8. Large volume with a declining CMF, anticipating the end of the downtrend to follow.
9. A gap pattern followed by rising CMF, a sign that price would continue upward.

> ✓ **Key Point**
>
> *Finding many signs confirming entry or exit is reassuring. But if you do not find such signs, that fact is just as valuable because it tells you to not act.*

In this chart, the confirmation signals, mostly based on clear candlestick signs and moves as well as other technical "red flags," were quite clear in their meaning. It is quite difficult to recognize a change in direction at the moment it occurs, which is why you cannot rely on candlesticks as your only indicators. When you use volume, CMF, and pattern changes such as gaps, your interpretation of candlesticks and timing of entry and exit will improve.

The Importance of Convergence and Divergence

Besides the easily spotted confirmations from technical price and volume changes, the trends in moving averages can also be extremely useful. The concepts of *convergence* and *divergence* help in identifying longer-term price direction and degrees of strength or weakness in those trends.

📖 Convergence/Divergence

The tendency for two long-term moving averages of price to move toward one another (converge) or away from one another (diverge).

Convergence signals a reduction in price volatility or the pending conclusion of a *primary trend* (bull or bear). Divergence signals increasing volatility and a growing trading range, or the beginning of a new primary trend.

📖 Primary Trend

The overall price direction in the market, either bull (upward) or bear (downward). Within each primary trend, offsetting secondary trends occur.

There are many ways to calculate moving averages, but in charting, the most popular combined averages are 200-session and 50-session moving averages. Chartists should be more concerned with the current trend than with the primary trend, recognizing that short-term price movement is where important swing action will generate profits. So in short-term trends as well as intermediate time periods, convergence and divergence play a different role than that associated with changes in the primary trend. Tracking the primary trend, convergence and divergence are seen as signals of coming long-term change. For swing traders, the importance of convergence and divergence is more immediate.

✓ Key Point

The convergence and divergence of two moving averages is a powerful trend signal; however, it often acts as a lagging and confirming indicator rather than as an immediate action point.

A lot of analysis is devoted to positive and negative crossover points. This analysis is based on the difference between the level of a moving average either above or below its moving average; however, swing traders can make use of the same crossover points to confirm candlestick-based indicators. In fact, the candlestick indicator is visible well before the convergence or divergence indicators, which are lagging indicators. With this in mind, the trend toward crossover is more important than the actual crossover itself. So when you see the moving averages converging, this action confirms what candlestick patterns have told you concerning reversal.

Some general observations can be made concerning moving averages in pairs (a 200-day and 50-day MA used together) and the relationship between the two. An additional series of observations can be made about the proximity and trend between moving averages and price:

1. When the shorter MA is above the longer, the trend is bullish.
2. When the shorter MA is below the longer, the trend is bearish.
3. When an MA remains lower than price levels, it signifies an uptrend.
4. When an MA remains above the price levels, it signifies a downtrend.
5. When the MA crosses the price (above in an uptrend or below in a downtrend), it signals a reversal.

Two important additional points to remember: First, moving averages are lagging indicators, so you are likely to use these trends as confirmation of what has already occurred in the candlestick pattern. Second, when tracking the relationship between MA and price, you may find contradiction of the preceding rules between two different MA moves. When this situation occurs, look for convergence as a signal of a change in the price trend.

For example, a three-month chart for Caterpillar (CAT) shows a number of valuable signals concerning MA as well as price. This three-month chart with the 50 MA and 200 MA is shown in Figure 8-3. The three-month period was very volatile for this company, covering a price range from a low of about $30 per share up to $48.

Chart courtesy of StockCharts.com

Figure 8-3 Moving averages with candlestick trends

Note the following significant points in analysis of the trend:

1. At the beginning of the chart, the 50 MA was below the 200 MA, which was bearish. Because the trends were converging, indication was that the bearish trend was coming to an end. However, one MA was above price and the other was below, which was a conflicting signal. The convergence pattern was more significant than proximity of either MA to price.

2. The 50 MA remained below price until mid-June, when it crossed. At the same time, the price downtrend continued. Based solely on the candlestick trend, the downtrend remained in effect based on the continuing proximity between the two MA lines.

3. Price levels reached their low at the beginning of July. The impending reversal was strongly confirmed by the convergence pattern and by the end of the candlestick downtrend ending with two short white candlesticks in three days in the second week of July.

4. The uptrend beginning July 13 was confirmed by several changes. First, repetitive price gaps (four in all) occurred over eight consecutive sessions. Second, the crossover in the MA lines occurred on July 20.

5. At the same point as the MA crossover, a large gap was seen. The two-day gap was even larger than the visible gap; the true gap was between opening price slightly above $35 on July 20 and the opening price at about $41 on the following day—a six-point gap.

6. Also on July 20, volume spiked, signaling continuation of the newly set uptrend.

7. With both MA lines below price, the uptrend was further confirmed.

Collectively, the price, candlestick patterns, MA lines, and volume all provide very strong signals throughout this chart. Swing traders relying strictly on candlestick patterns might have been uncertain at several points in this chart without the confirmation of the MA lines. However, it is also important to realize that primary reliance has to remain on the candlesticks because the MA trends are lagging. Developments including the rapidly converging MA lines in the first half of the chart strongly anticipated the downtrend. However, the crossover of the two MA lines lags behind the more apparent end of the downtrend and start of the uptrend a week earlier. The relationship between change in trend and crossover in the MA lines is apparent in hindsight, but at the time, the entry and exit signals were equally strong and visible.

> ✓ **Key Point**
>
> *The MA trends confirm previous decisions at crossover points. However, they are most useful when the convergence or divergence trend is taking place where candlestick entry or exit is observed before crossover actually takes place.*

Primary Trends and Candlestick-Based Entry or Exit

Timing of entry and exit is always the key to swing trading. Recognition of a short-term trend is fairly easy, but knowing (a) when a reversal is coming and (b) when a continuation pattern is underway are more elusive interpretive skills. Although swing trading is invariably based on very short-term trends, the primary trend underway at the time defines the likelihood of a short-term trend's duration within that longer-term trend.

In a bullish primary trend, by definition, the interim uptrends are likely to be longer lasting and cover a greater number of points than the contracting downtrends that will occur as well. In a bearish primary trend, the opposite is true: short-term downtrends are going to move faster and cover more points, and offsetting short-term uptrends will be weaker and of shorter duration. This general observation is important intelligence for swing traders. Awareness of the primary trend is going to help you judge the current price movement and improve your timing even more than you can by relying on specific signals in the chart patterns.

Swing traders who rely on the many entry and exit signals found in short-term price movement, notably in candlestick signs, moves, and patterns, can overcome the dilemma every trader faces. How do you know when a specific directional change in price is a momentary pause or a reversal? How can you tell when a strong single-day movement is a sign of continuation or exhaustion? In many instances, the signals are not conclusive and you need to rely on your judgment. Swing traders are wise to follow one general rule: when you cannot read a signal, get out and stay out until the picture clears. If you are already in a position and the signals are unclear, refer to the primary trend. If you are in a bull market and an uptrend is underway, chances are good that a conflicting signal to the upside means continuation, and in a bear market, a conflicting signal to the downside means continuation. The same general assumption is applied to reversal patterns as well.

> ✓ **Key Point**
>
> *Perhaps the best rule for swing trading is: when you are not sure of a signal, stay away. Don't act until the signal is more definitive.*

During the bull market of the summer of 2009, differences between short-term uptrends and downtrends were noticeable. For example, the three-month chart of Kraft Foods (KFT) displayed noticeable differences in the duration and scope of short-term trends, as shown in Figure 8-4.

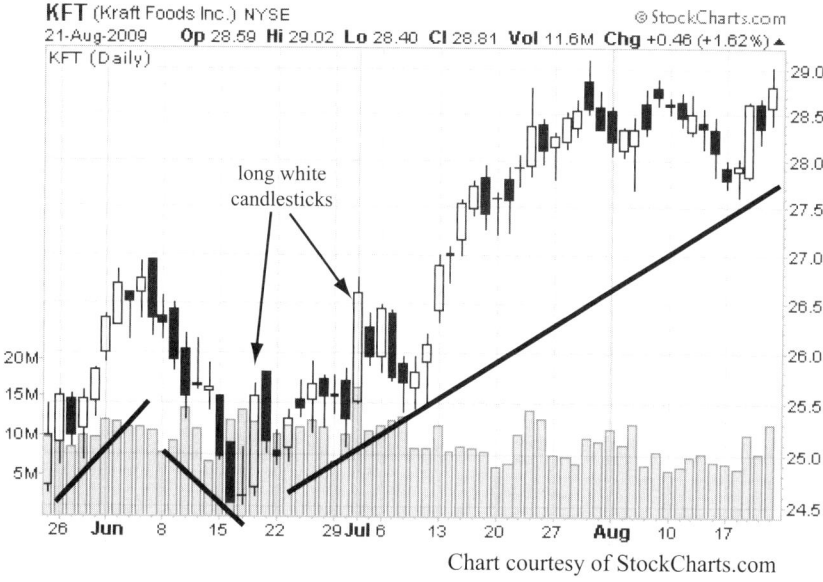

Chart courtesy of StockCharts.com

Figure 8-4 Short-term trends within the primary trend

Kraft went through some short-term movement involving an uptrend and then a downtrend, each covering only about a two-point price range. However, this entire period was part of a primary bull market trend, which is one reason that the final uptrend lasted at least two months, to the end of the chart. A second point of interest: the beginning of the longer-term uptrend was signaled by the two occurrences of long white days. The first followed a doji at the bottom of the previous downtrend and represented an exceptionally bullish reversal. The second was yet another setup for the coming uptrend, which was further confirmed by the price gaps in subsequent sessions. This pattern set up a new, higher trading range with support at 27.75 and resistance at 29.

Another chart covering the same period shows how candlestick signs—especially very strong signs—signal longer-term price movement within the primary trend. The three-month chart for Merck (MRK) is shown in Figure 8-5.

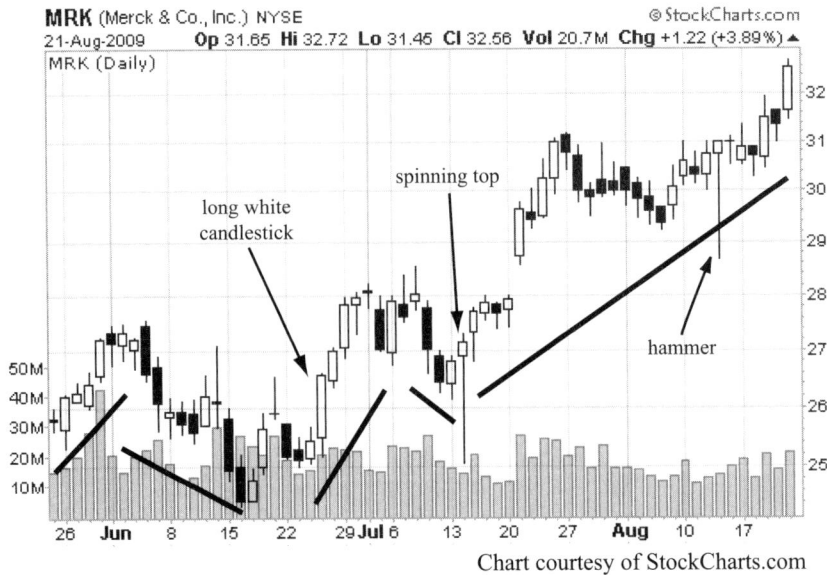

Figure 8-5 Short-term trends with strong candlestick signals

This chart is especially interesting because the trends are characterized by some very strong single-day candlestick signs. The first half of the chart consisted of a series of brief and small-duration trends as marked. The last of the short-term uptrends was signaled by a long white candlestick, a very bullish short-term indicator followed by three additional uptrend days. This typical swing trading pattern was followed by a doji and then a fairly typical downtrend. The marked spinning top was a strong bullish signal that started a much longer-term and stronger uptrend, confirmed by the gap pattern five sessions later. Recall that a white candle with a long lower shadow indicates that an attempt by sellers to bring the price down on that session failed, and the longer the lower shadow, the more bullish the sign.

This uptrend was later marked by another important one-day candle, the hammer. This unusual candlestick can either be bullish or bearish, depending on context and on what actually follows. If it is a true hammer during the uptrend, it is a continuation indicator. If the price had moved downward, it would have told you that this was a hanging man, a bearish reversal signal. In this pattern, the color of the real body is not as important as the context and what patterns follow.

✓ Key Point

Some candlestick signs, such as the hammer or hanging man, can be either bullish or bearish depending on its placement in the existing trend. It may be either a continuation or reversal signal.

Another confirming factor is that this candlestick occurs within a larger primary trend, indicating a greater likelihood that price will, in fact, continue upward. Looking at the continuation of this chart over the following few months, this indication was confirmed. Merck continued in its upward movement for the following four months, as shown in Figure 8-6.

Chart courtesy of StockCharts.com

Figure 8-6 Price direction confirmed within a primary trend

This chart demonstrates that, in fact, the previously referenced sign was a hammer because price trended upward afterward. This chart also supports the contention that short-term uptrends tend to be stronger during primary bull trends (and vice versa in bear markets). For the first three months of this chart, support holds firm while resistance gradually rises. This period is also characterized by the pattern swing traders like: a series of short uptrends and downtrends within a four-point range. However, note the exceptionally strong bullish signal at the beginning of November. At the conclusion of the latest downtrend, a very high volume spike occurs, followed immediately by a long white candle. This anticipates the remainder of the chart, with a strong uptrend moving from the low point of about 30.25 up to 37.75 at the high point. The candlestick signals were strong throughout this and the preceding chart and were confirmed with subsequent candlestick trends as well as the single-volume spike.

Setup Criteria and Action Points

Every chart watcher seeks reliable entry and exit signals. However, swing traders may not always be aware of one important point worth remembering: entry and exit signals are not always identical. If they were, you would assume that a proper indication will always tell you to exit one position and, at the same time, enter another. For example, if you have bought shares at the bottom of a downtrend, what happens when the resulting reversal and uptrend concludes? You would expect to acknowledge the exit signal and sell shares, but then go short in anticipation of another downtrend.

> ✓ **Key Point**
>
> *Be sure to identify the difference between concurrent exit/entry signals and exit signals alone, which often are followed by a period of consolidation.*

In some situations, the end of a trend does not signal reversal, but consolidation. If price movement will be sideways for several sessions, it could imply that when prices move once again, this movement will most likely be in the opposite direction. However, it is equally possible that prices will continue in the same direction following a pause in the trend. In this case, an exit setup signal is *not* also an entry signal for the opposite price movement.

The similarities between entry and exit signals reveal that in many cases, entry and exit are identical—but not always. When you see *exit*, you do not always see *entry* indicated at the same time. A comparison between the sets of signals makes this point, notably when two or more of the signals occur together:

Entry Signals

End of the trend via a narrow-range day (NRD), also known as a doji

Reversal candles such as long-legged doji, spinning top, or marubozu

High volume

Gapping patterns near beginning of the trend

Technical indicator changes, such as CMF or MA convergence and cross-over

Exit Signals

End of the trend lasting three sessions or more via different-colored candles

Long-legged doji or spinning top, especially in conjunction with a marubozu

Gapping pattern including intraday gaps, near the end of the trend

Technical indicator changes, such as CMF or MA divergence

Many of the signals are similar or identical; the key is to find confirming indicators of the same meanings, either entry or exit (or both). But the differences may be subtle. For example, price gaps are among the strongest of swing trading signals. Some points to remember:

1. *Intraday gaps are often invisible.* The importance of gaps often is missed because they take place between sessions. The difference between yesterday's close and today's open might include overlapping real bodies, but significant gaps as well. The six types of overnight gapping patterns are shown in the preceding chapter (refer to Figure 7-5) and are worth reviewing.

2. *Gaps occurring after a trend is established, moving in the same direction, may signal exhaustion and an impending end to the trend, thus an exit signal.* One of the strongest signs that the current short-term trend is coming to an end is a gap in the trend direction. This sign is not easy to distinguish from a continuation pattern, which is why you need to confirm the indicator with other candlestick or technical measures, notably basic signs like support and resistance, head and shoulders, or top/bottom repetitive tests over an extended period. The exhaustion signal often follows tests or stops right at the border of the trading range.

3. *Gaps occurring at or near the beginning of a trend and moving in the trend direction may signal that the new trend is genuine and will continue; thus, this serves as an entry signal.* When you see one trend end and another begin, gaps can take on a different meaning than exhaustion. A continuation gap is most likely to take place at or near the beginning of the trend. So if an uptrend starts out with a gap close to support, or a downtrend starts with a gap near resistance, you have to accept the premise that the trading range provides "movement room" for the trend to develop. Given separate technical confirmation, gaps at the beginning of trend are strong indicators supporting the current price direction.

> ✓ **Key Point**
>
> *Price gaps, including those between trading sessions, are very strong and important signals, but depending on where they occur within the trend and within proximity to the support or resistance levels, they can have different meanings.*

All reversal signals have to be generalizations because for every rule of charting, you can find the notable exception. However, gaps often are present when entry signals are not found at the same point as exit signals. In some instances, exit signals stand alone without the requisite entry signals, and they may be followed with either continuation of the previous trend or a reversal. For example, in Figure 8-7, the quarterly chart of Apple (AAPL) reverses a consolidation period followed by a continuation of the previous trend.

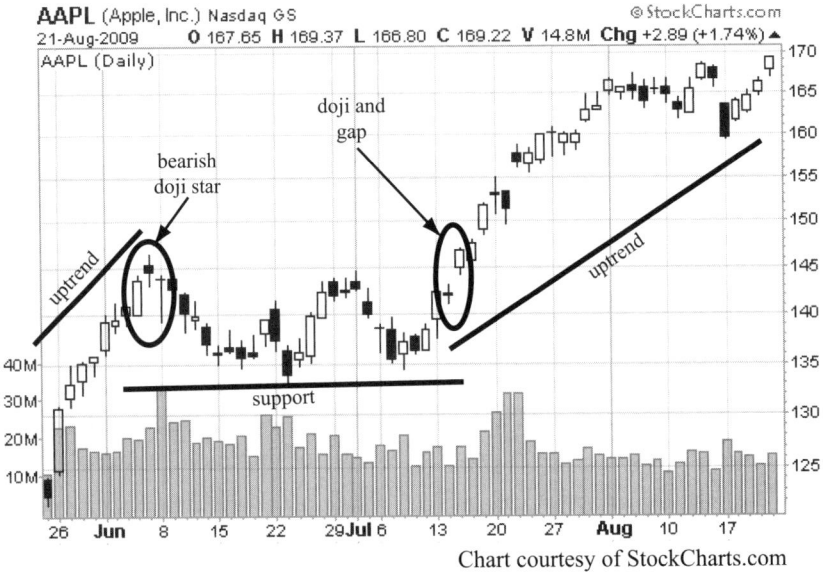

Figure 8-7 Exit signals followed by continuation

Note that the period of consolidation does not fall below support. The initial uptrend contains an exit signal with the bearish doji star shown on the chart. This is a very strong three-stick pattern consisting of an upward day, an upward gap, a doji, a downward gap, and then a downward day. At this point there was no specific entry signal present. The second uptrend is established and confirmed by the combination of a gap at the top and then a spinning top, as highlighted.

Of course, an established trend will not always continue after a pause, as in this example. Some pauses in the trend are followed by strong reversal trends, and there is no way to know in advance which outcome will follow. So an exit signal without the requisite entry signal requires waiting out the consolidation before moving, based on the fact that price could move in either direction. For example, the three-month chart for DuPont (DD) contains this pattern and trend, as shown in Figure 8-8.

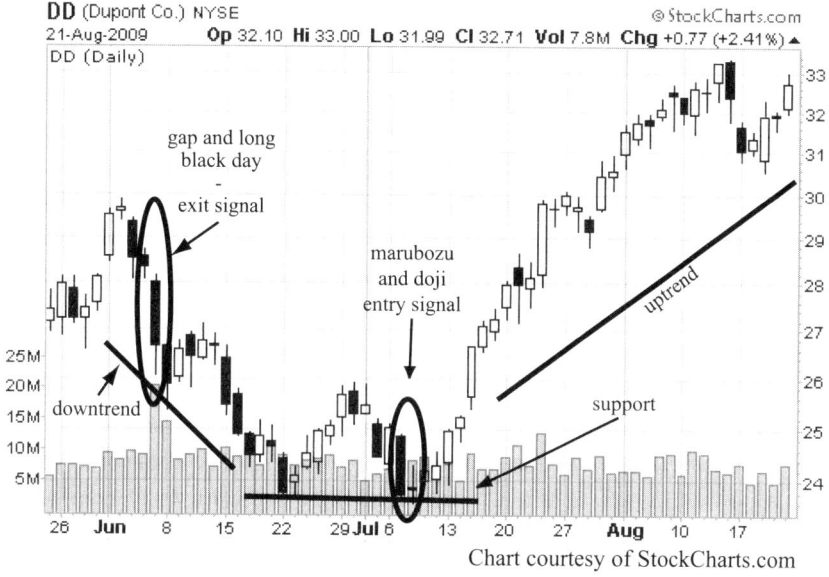

Figure 8-8 Exit signals followed by reversal

This chart contains many interesting signals. The downtrend at the beginning of the chart is set by the topping gaps but confirmed by the downward long black day immediately after a *second* downward gap. The exit signal for the downtrend occurs when three consecutive down days are followed by a white day, which sets off the period of consolidation lasting about one month.

Note how the support level is tested twice immediately before the uptrend begins. Even without observation of candlestick patterns or other technical indicators, the strength of the newly set support level and the double test of the bottom are strong indicators on their own. However, the combined black marubozu and doji. Normally, a black marubozu would serve as a bearish signal, but what follows really determines its significance. In this case, the doji (or in swing trading language, the NRD) in the following session is a warning that the preceding day may not be bearish at all. In fact, the doji is an entry signal that is rapidly followed by eight uptrend sessions, half of which include gaps. Because these gaps occur as the trend begins, they strongly confirm the entry signal. In this case, a downtrend is followed by a period of consolidation, and then an uptrend.

> ✓ **Key Point**
>
> Gaps found at the beginning of a trend initiated near support (for uptrends) or resistance (for downtrends) are likely to confirm the direction. Those occurring at or near the end of a trend and approaching support or resistance imply exhaustion and anticipate reversal.

This chart also serves as a good example of how traditional technical indicators can work nicely with confirming candlestick patterns. The double test of support may have been enough for a chartist to call the reversal; when support is tested in this way, it often precedes a strong uptrend. However, it does not always occur. The candlestick signals not only are strong indicators on their own merit (especially with the uptrend gaps), but also confirm the expected price movement after the double bottom.

Selling Short in Swing Trades

Clearly, swing traders have to be aware that entry and exit coexist at times, but not always. There are times when exit is clear, but entry has not yet emerged. Swing traders face another dilemma, however: to trade both sides of the swing, they need to be able not only to go long at the bottom, but also to go short at the top.

A great number of traders, probably a majority, avoid short selling due to the complexity, cost, and risk involved. Shorting stock is not a moderate strategy; as a consequence, many swing traders seek entry at the bottom and exit at the top, but avoid the other side of the swing cycle. When you short stock, you have to borrow shares from your broker and then sell them. As long as the short position remains open, you have to pay interest to your broker for the borrowed shares. You face considerable risk as long as you are short; if you time the entry correctly and stock prices continue to rise instead of falling, you lose. Eventually, you may need to cover the short at a loss. In the ideal trade, prices do fall and you can cover at a profit.

Some swing traders limit their long-side risk by employing fewer than 100 shares of stock. You can swing trade with a smaller number for very little added cost, so this approach makes sense. However, shorting fewer than 100 shares of stock might not be possible. It is understandable that short sellers will avoid shorting for all these reasons. However, there is a practical and affordable alternative: using options for downside swings.

> ✓ **Key Point**
> The risk, cost, and complexity of selling short restrict many swing traders to uptrends only. This means they miss out of one-half of all swing trading opportunities.

Rules of the options market are particularly complex and special, and no one should employ any options strategies without experience and practice. However, for those who do understand options, their use for swing trading is flexible and actually reduces risks. A *put* is an option granting its owner the right (but not the obligation) to sell 100 shares of an underlying stock. So instead of selling short, you can *buy* a put and accomplish the same swing trading posture. As the stock's price declines, the put's value increases. This is one of the rare instances in which it makes sense to buy puts that will expire in less than one month. Under most strategies involving long options, you need to keep positions open long enough for price changes to develop, meaning you have to pay for *time value* as well. But in swing trading, you expect a trend to develop over as little as three trading sessions.

Every option gives you control over 100 shares of stock. With this fact in mind, there are many possible swing trading combinations you can use on both sides of the swing. They include

1. Buying calls at the bottom and buying puts at the top.
2. Selling calls at the top and buying calls at the bottom. (This is a practical system, especially when you also own 100 shares of the underlying stock, so that the short call is covered, making this a very conservative strategy.)
3. Selling puts at the bottom and buying puts at the top. (Selling puts is higher risk than buying, but as one possible swing trading strategy, shorting the put produces cash income, and when the signal is exceptionally strong for an uptrend, the risks are mitigated.)
4. Selling puts at the bottom and selling calls at the top. (This is a completely credit-based strategy, meaning you earn money on both sides, further reducing the price-spread risk. If you own 100 shares, the short call risk is very low.)

Options make swing trading very flexible, but for much lower costs. Long options cost only a fraction of the 100 shares they allow you to control, as little as 5 to 10 percent of the price for 100 shares. However, long positions also limit risk. You can never lose more than the relatively small price of the option. With their low cost, you can diversify among several different stocks at the same time using options in place of stock as a swing trading mechanism.

> ✓ **Key Point**
> Swing trading with options instead of stock improves flexibility and diversification while reducing risk. However, no one should consider using options in any strategy unless he completely understands how they work.

The complexity of options and their selection criteria demand a lot of study. Risk levels vary greatly between long and short positions and depending on whether or not those short positions are covered or uncovered. Another risk factor is the price distance between the fixed strike of the option and the current price of the stock. In other words, there are many points to keep in mind when trading options. They are exceptionally powerful tools for swing trading, but only if you are a seasoned options trader.

Whether you trade in shares of stock or option contracts, the entire system for timing of entry and exit relies on your skill in spotting and using trends. This is the subject of the next chapter.

chapter 9

Spotting Trends and Using Trendlines

Candlesticks provide intelligence on two levels. First, they help you to determine what is happening at the moment and what price direction is likely in the next handful of trading sessions. Second, they provide insight into the current trend—its strength or weakness, likelihood of continuation or reversal, and duration.

Candlesticks can be used by themselves to time entry and exit. However, they are even more powerful as timing tools when viewed in a larger context of long-term chart analysis. Swing traders, for example, rely on very short-term trends and expect three- to five-day price movement followed by reversal. The process of finding and acting on entry and exit setup signals is continual and is based on an observation that most traders overreact, causing prices to move too far within a limited time span.

This belief is well founded in most cases. However, it does not address the problem of longer-term trends. Some trends continue in one direction for weeks or even months. This is especially true when stocks have remained within an extended sideways trading pattern for weeks at a time. The need for prices to move upward or downward becomes pent up at such times and could lead to an unusually long and unbroken trend of considerable time. In uncertain markets, swing traders will note that the common emotions of greed and fear that dominate short-term price movement are probably augmented. However, these conditions also create uncertainty when price movement suddenly breaks away from the sideways trend and moves either upward or downward for a long time.

As long as continuation signals are found in candlestick formations, it is possible to ride a trend for as long as it lasts. However, it is also difficult to accurately judge the meaning of some candlestick formations in such long-term trending patterns. This is where additional confirmation tools are required. Candlesticks work well only when prices go through typical short-term waves of change. When momentum is exceptionally strong, candlestick formations require more confirmation than ever. The best confirmation is achieved by combining candlestick formations with continuation or reversal signs you find in trendline analysis.

The many technical indicators popularly used by chartists to identify price trends are valuable, but when they confirm what the candlesticks reveal, their accuracy is increased significantly. Even when momentum is stronger than interim technical signals, the process of signal and confirmation is crucial for accurate timing of entry and exit.

Candlesticks remain a primary early indicator of what is going on in the pattern. The formations come is three distinct types. The single candlestick of significance (such as the doji or marubozu) is a sign. A two-stick series such as engulfing patterns and the harami is defined as a move. And finally, a candlestick formation of three candlesticks such as three white soldiers or the morning star sets up a pattern. Collectively, the visual price patterns of candlesticks contribute to the trend itself, but candlestick formations are not trends. A *trend* is the direction in which prices move and is distinguished by momentum and either strengthening or weakening tendencies over time. Candlesticks do not specifically identify trends but are most valuable for spotting continuation and reversal, especially within a current trendline.

Identifying the Trendline

A trend is a well-known phenomenon in stock prices. Those prices—whether seen in individual stocks or in market indices—tend to continue moving in an established direction for a period of time before it stops and reverses. This tendency of *reversion to the mean* is a statistical reference. It tells you that when prices move away from their longer-term average, the tendency is for price to reverse and move back toward that mean.

> ✓ **Key Point**
>
> *No trend continues forever. Eventually, the current direction stops and begins moving back toward the longer-term average.*

📖 Reversion to the Mean

A tendency for prices to reverse course and move back toward their longer-term average.

The concept is important in chart analysis. Anyone who has studied chart patterns over time has recognized that the faster price moves beyond its trading range, the more likely it is to exhaust that trend and reverse. Fast price movement is seen in repetitive price gaps, breakouts, and higher-than-average volatility You are also likely to see an increase in unusual candlestick signs such as longer-than-average days, consecutive doji moves, and misleading or contradictory signals. Those are signs that trends are concluding. You can put to good use the simple realization that no trend is going to last forever by looking for changes in an established trendline.

The statistical observation expressed in reversion to the mean tells you that prices *tend* to follow the averages. So when you are observing price in conjunction with a 200-day and a 50-day moving average, you assign great importance to the distance between price and the two averages. The statistical rule tells you in addition that the greater the distance price moves away from the mean, the higher the chances that reversion will soon occur. This is not just a theory; it is also a reality. It is easily observed in a series of coin tosses, for example. You know that there is a 50–50 chance of either heads or tails coming up. However, every toss is independent, so there is no assurance that a trend will develop. Even so, if the toss comes up "heads" eight times in a row, you know that the 50–50 odds have wandered substantially away from the average you expect. For that reason alone, you would expect to see "tails" come up soon. Every toss is independent, but the odds of tails are still at 50–50.

The theory of reversion to the mean tells you that no trend is going to continue indefinitely. Eventually, every trend ends and turns back toward the moving averages. This outcome is inevitable because stock prices, like all *trends*, rely on interaction between buyers and sellers, the two moving forces behind price. If price moves too high, stockholders will seek an exit and will sell. If prices move too low, traders will seek a bargain price and will buy. This unending interaction is going to show up in a series of changes in trendlines. These changes are not difficult to spot. They may consist of

1. *A weakening or breakdown of the line*. The most visible sign is a change in the direction of the trend, which is expressed in a violation of a trendline. As long as the line continues moving upward with evolving support or resistance, the trend continues. However, eventually price is going to

reverse, even slightly. This reversal is often a sign that the trendline is concluding. However, because short-term price movement is always chaotic, you need confirmation from other technical indicators, or from candlestick patterns indicating reversal.

A trendline is a powerful tool because it tracks evolving support or resistance. As price levels rise or fall, they often tend to remain within the same breadth of trading, making the trading range easily definable. The range is rarely stationary. The tendency is for price trends to generally move while the distance between resistance and support moves as well, but without expanding or contracting. When the trading range changes as price levels evolve, triangles, wedges, and pennants form and take on significance separate from the trendline. When such indicators counter the trendline direction, they may provide early signs that the current trend is narrowing and will soon stop and reverse direction.

> ✓ **Key Point**
>
> *Trendlines make support and resistance visible even when the trading range is evolving as part of a long-term trend.*

2. *Candlestick formations that anticipate reversal.* The best-known and most-visible types of candlestick formations signal reversal. Confirmation of this reversal occurs in several ways. One way is a reversal indicated by one candlestick sign, move, or pattern, followed immediately by another that also anticipates reversal. A second confirming sign is a violation of the trendline, even a small or momentary one. You expect to see trendlines hold consistently. Any drop below an ascending support level or a rise above a declining resistance level is a subtle but important warning sign that the whole trend may reverse. This is similar in strength to the better-known head-and-shoulders pattern, which tests resistance or support and then sees prices move in the opposite direction.

Another way that candlestick formations are confirmed is through outside changes such as volume spikes, consecutive price gaps, or important reversals in CMF and other technical indicators. Converging or diverging moving averages further support what the candlestick formations anticipate. There is no shortage of potential conforming signs in support of what the candlesticks tell you. Unfortunately, there may be so many that you observe both confirming and contradictory signs at the same time. When this situation occurs, you may rely the most on what two indicators reveal: candlestick formations and the signs in the current trendline.

3. *Other technical changes.* In so many trendline indicators, you find confirmation not only through the specific candlestick formations, but also through what longer-range technical indicators emerge. For example, a trendline may be characterized by a strong movement culminating in numerous price gaps. They may be reversal gaps that warn you of the reversal before the trendline itself turns around. This situation may occur when momentum of the trend carries price to the level of being overbought or oversold. When momentum trumps other technical signs, it may shield the impending reversal from view. At such times, look for technical signs in the form of CMF changes, moving average convergence and divergence, and repeated but unsuccessful tests of resistance and support. These signs may all occur even as the trendline appears to be holding steady.

Pay special attention to tests of resistance and support. One of the widely observed "rules" of chart analysis is that trading always remains within the trading range ... until it breaks out of the trading range. In other words, resistance and support are truly the "lines in the sand" of trends, and when a breakthrough takes place, it may signal a fast change in price or may exhaust and reverse the "rule" of resistance and support for a long period of time and then break out. Check the trendline as well as candlestick patterns. The breakout is a red flag that price is going to move rapidly, but you may not be able to tell in which direction. This is the point at which the trendline, supported by candlestick formations, can be the most revealing indicator.

> ✓ **Key Point**
>
> *The breakout signal is difficult to interpret; it may signal a strong price movement or impending reversal. At such times, the trendline can help to determine which price direction will rule.*

A distinction should be made between the trend and the *trendline*. They are not necessarily the same, even though they usually are seen at the same time. The trendline is a readily seen, visible straight line connecting a series of ascending or descending price levels. In candlestick analysis, the trendline normally is drawn just above and just below the daily price range (as opposed to opening and closing prices). In other words, the line is higher than upper shadows in a downward movement, or lower than the lower shadows of an upward price movement. A study of trendlines often anticipates a change in direction or weakening of the current trend. In technical analysis, a broadening or narrowing trendline (known variously as the triangle, wedge, or pennant) signals either a strengthening of the current trend or its impending conclusion.

📖 Trendline

A series of straight lines bordering the highest and lowest point in a current price trend.

For example, the six-month chart for Hewlett-Packard (HPQ) revealed a steady rise in price levels, as shown in Figure 9-1. This trendline was confirmed not so much by outside technical indicators, but by the *lack* of any warning signs of impending reversal. On-balance volume tracked the uptrend well, and CMF revealed two dips below the bull/bear line, but both were weak and neither lasted long. In other words, the trendline lasted many months and did not show any signs of weakening, even with a 50 percent increase in price.

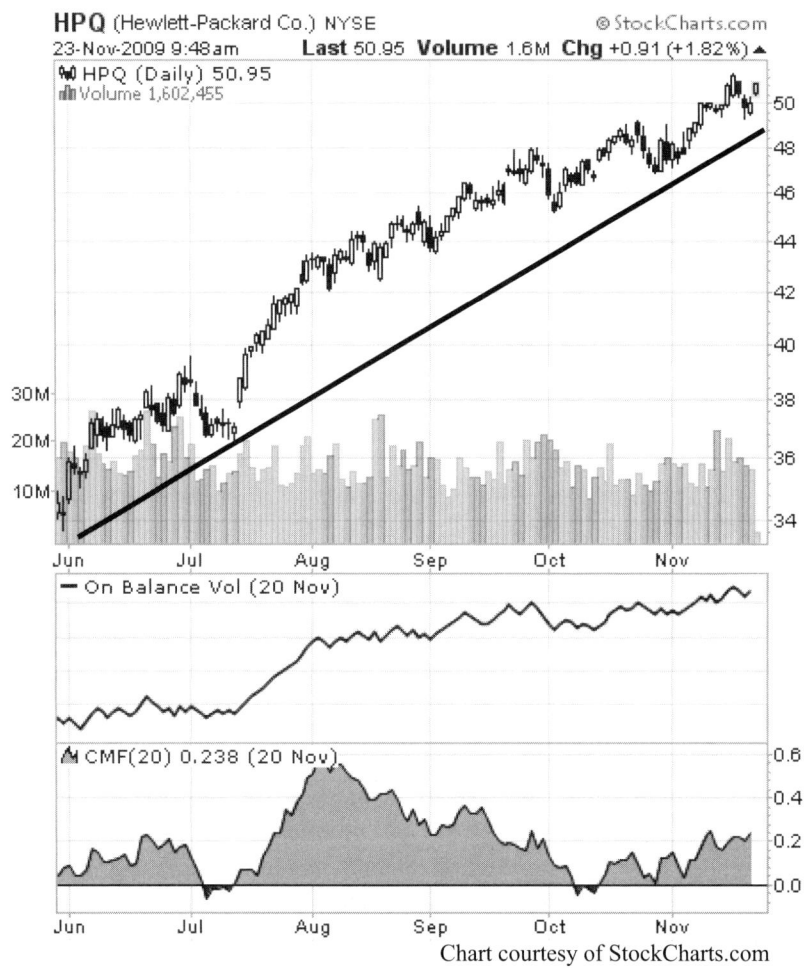

Chart courtesy of StockCharts.com

Figure 9-1 Trendline in an uptrend

When prices are on the rise, as in this case, the trendline is usually shown along the line of support. When prices are falling, the trendline is drawn above, tracking the line of resistance. The quarterly chart for Exxon-Mobil (XOM), shown in Figure 9-2, revealed two distinct downtrends, each lasting about one month.

✓ Key Point

Trendlines provide a context for defining price movement and an orderly trading range. The end of the trendline is invariably confirmed with candlestick formations, often very strong ones.

Chart courtesy of StockCharts.com

Figure 9-2 Trendline in a downtrend

The point here is to show how trendlines appear and are marked. Also note how clearly the beginning and end of each reversal were marked. The first downtrend was signaled by a prominent doji day at the top and then confirmed by a black marubozu three sessions later. The short reversal ended quickly and was signaled by the three-day price gaps. (The first was quite visible; the second showed up with the black candle followed by the white; and the third was even more subtle, the gap between the white candle with the long lower shadow followed by the black candle.)

The downtrend ended with a large gap followed by a doji, and a subsequent strong uptrend was characterized by numerous gaps. This trendline tells you that the uptrend would not last for long; it ended up running for two weeks and concluded with the doji and price decline. The final downtrend clearly concluded with the very long white candle, a second white candle, and then a gap before the final session of the chart appeared.

The trends in this quarterly chart extended over only a 10-point range. However, when you watch trendlines and also see confirming candlestick reversal signals, it does not matter what point spread is involved. The key issue in these charts is how the trendlines track the change and also how candlestick formations flag the reversal points.

Trendlines and Candlesticks as Confirmation

A trendline helps to locate and confirm reversal points in the trend. In fact, when a trendline weakens, it may be better visual proof of a coming reversal than many other, more popular indicators. When you see that the existing trendline is confirmed by candlesticks providing the same clues (bullish formations in a bullish trendline and bearish formations in a bullish trendline), that trendline is an excellent form of information that the trend is continuing. When you see emerging opposite indicators (such as bearish candlesticks in a bullish trendline or bullish candlesticks in a bearish trendline), they are early signs of reversal.

> ✓ **Key Point**
>
> *When trendlines are compared with candlestick indicators, it is much easier to determine whether the current tendency is toward continuation or reversal.*

For example, the quarterly chart for Caterpillar (CAT) demonstrated how a weakening trendline is confirmed—in this case, very strongly—by candlestick formations. The chart is shown in Figure 9-3.

9 Spotting Trends and Using Trendlines

Figure 9-3 Downward trendline ending

The initial downtrend was short-lived and paused with a small price rise topped with two doji days. This scenario could be interpreted as an early indication that the downtrend was weakening and about to end. However, the downtrend resumed and continued for a few more sessions. The strong sign that a reversal was about to take place was found in two candlestick bullish reversals: the first, a harami cross; and the second—occurring immediately after—a morning star. The two-day move and the three-day pattern were both strong bullish signals on their own; occurring next to one another was an exceptionally strong reversal indicator. The resulting strong uptrend, marked by the bullish trendline, contained numerous upside gaps that continued until a particularly strong gap and black day. However, that black day ended up as the first session of a second harami cross, this one even stronger than the first. This tells the analyst that the uptrend had not yet ended. The strong trendline supported this interpretation of the trend's continuation, which did not pause until the last leg of the chart.

You may find equally compelling confirmation when uptrends end. For example, the quarterly chart of McDonald's (MCD), shown in Figure 9-4, provides a very strong candlestick sign that the uptrend has come to an end.

Figure 9-4 Upward trendline ending

In this example, a volatile recent price history ran through to the third week in June, where the trendline appeared to be setting a new bottom. As prices began moving upward around the third week of July (including white days with gaps), there was no immediate indication that the upward momentum was ending. However, note the last white candlestick day before the large downward gap. The long upper shadow revealed that buyers were not able to drive prices further upward; the day ended with a narrow space between the opening and closing price. This was the first sign of coming trouble and of the absolute end to the upward-moving trendline.

> ✓ **Key Point**
>
> *Even a subtle indicator, such as an isolated shadow at the top or bottom of the trend, ends up being the best indicator of a strong reversal. When confirmed by a change in the trendline, the reversal can be quite strong.*

Confirmation of this end involved two parts. First was the large downward gap, and second was the combined long black day with exceptional spike in volume. This scenario set up the downward trendline that followed. This chart does not provide enough subsequent information to tell whether the newly established downtrend would be strong enough to continue. Later price movement showed, in fact, that prices ended up rising to $64 per share. However, on the limited information provided in the three-month chart of MCD, the reversal in trendline was confirmed by the three clear signals (large upper shadow on the last white day, large downward gap, and volume spike on a long black candle day).

The trendline does not have to be especially strong to confirm the trend or, equally revealing, to point to the weakening of that trend. Trendline duration can be further confirmed by commonly appearing bullish or bearish candlestick formations that indicate continuation. These formations include neck lines, thrusting lines, or meeting lines confirming patterns in either direction, and ongoing moving averages without signs of impending convergence. Reversal patterns include gaps, MA convergence, changes in CMF or on-balance volume, exceptional volume spikes, doji patterns (especially consecutive doji days), and large gaps indicating exhaustion of the trend.

Applying Moving Averages to Candlestick Analysis

A trend or trendline is easily visible on most charts. However, some charts also demonstrate exceptional volatility, making it impossible to use price alone to understand whether the current price is in a continuation mode or about to reverse. In these instances, you can use moving averages—and especially a visible converging pattern—to augment price analysis.

For example, Johnson & Johnson (JNJ) was a difficult chart to read over the six-month period shown in Figure 9-5. As soon as a candlestick formation implied movement in one direction, it was contradicted by a different formation in the other. With price alone, this was not an easy chart to read. However, when a 200-day and 50-day moving average were overlaid, the picture cleared up.

> ✓ *Key Point*
> *Some trends are hard to read or even impossible to spot. At such times, a study of moving average lines can be the best indicator or confirmation available.*

Figure 9-5 Moving averages to support trends

At the beginning of this chart, the price trend was unsettled and unclear. However, at the same time the 200-day MA was falling and the 50-day MA was rising. This pattern anticipated a crossover in the near future. This converging pattern was bullish because when the shorter-term MA is above the longer-term MA, it demonstrates upward momentum.

If you wait for crossover to occur, you often are too late to take advantage of the directional indication. Observing the convergence, you could anticipate upward price movement even though clear confirmation from candlestick patterns was not strong. A series of three or more white candlesticks toward the end of June and beginning of July provided some indication of stronger upward momentum, but prices did not begin rising until crossover by mid-July. At this point, you would seek out a weakening of the trendline, which appears to show up by mid-August. At this point, prices have paused and a series of consecutive black candlestick days appear. Still, the indication is not strong enough by itself. However, the divergence between the two MA lines continues to widen at this point, which is an early indication that price must soon retreat back toward the average (revert to the mean). The combination of the pause in the trendline and the divergence between the two MA lines indicates that prices may be topping out. In fact, from the end of August through the end of November, the MA trends slowed down and the gap between the MA lines remained fairly constant. Prices remained in a sideways pattern between $58 and $62 per share before rallying to $65 by the end of December.

✓ Key Point

Convergence and divergence are excellent confirming signals, but they should not be relied on as the sole means for timing entry or exit.

You may further confirm the moving averages using another technical indicator: the reaching of a new high or new low price based on the last 52 weeks. The marketwide indicator is used to support the existing trend. As new highs increase, the signs are bullish; and as new lows increase, the signs are bearish. However, when a new high or new low is seen on an individual stock, it has to be analyzed in context, based on several factors:

1. *Comparison to the overall market.* When the overall trend is firmly set, stocks may tend to follow suit, even if the individual technical indicators are weak or contradictory. However, this tendency is also most likely to be adjusted after traders realize that the market momentum has created an overbought or oversold condition in the stock.

2. *Placement within the current trend.* The trend and trendline are the most revealing portions of price momentum and movement. Candlestick formations are short term and serve to pinpoint reversals (or continuation) in the trend itself. So when a stock's price reaches a 52-week high or low, it has to be judged in the context of the existing trend. Has the trend topped or bottomed out with the 52-week price level? Is the trendline still strong or is it weakening?

3. *Sustainability of the record price level.* Momentum eventually reaches an end, known among traders as exhaustion. So the big question for the new high or new low point is whether or not it can be sustained. The combined visual signals of trendline and candlestick formations will define the

sustainability of the current price level, whether at the top or at the bottom of the 52-week history.

4. *Proximity to resistance and support of the new price and of recent price movement.* Some stocks remain within a clearly defined trading range over many months, whereas others maintain the same breadth of range while price levels evolve, either upward or downward. Thus, a new top might not violate resistance, and a new bottom might not be below support. In these cases, proximity to the borders of the trading range without a breakthrough imply that the range is likely to continue holding. When the new high or new low is a price breakthrough, refer to trendlines and candlestick formations to confirm technical signals. This is the best way to determine whether the breakthrough will continue or reverse and fill.

5. *Frequency of new high or new low.* Is this the first time in 52 weeks that a new high or low price level has been reached? That would be significant. However, if price levels are evolving, it is possible that a new 52-week record is being set repetitively. Remember, the 52-week price record is a form of moving average. If the stock's price is going through a long-term bull or bear trend, you may see numerous record high or low prices. The distinction between the number of new price records is one way to define the significance of the indicator.

6. *Recent price volatility of the stock.* If a new high or new low shows up in a stock with low volatility, that is probably far more significant than for a stock with high volatility. By definition, high-volatility stocks have to be expected to continually violate previously set trading ranges. The problem is that in these situations, identifying an emerging trend is quite difficult, even with good candlestick formations and short-term trendlines. Higher-volatility patterns make all forms of analysis more difficult. The good news is that even the most volatile stocks eventually settle down and begin to conform to widely recognized technical "rules" and trends.

The many ways that signals can be recognized and confirmed invariably return to the use of candlestick signs, moves, and patterns as a primary and leading source for reversal (as well as for continuation). However, candlesticks are only the first step in locating the point where entry and exit make the most sense. You still need to rely on additional technical indicators, especially the most favorite ones, to confirm what the candlesticks indicate to you. The next chapter studies many of the technical indicators that are most useful as confirmation of trends you first see in candlestick formations.

chapter 10

Technical Indicators

In all the preceding chapters, candlestick signs, moves, and patterns on actual stock charts were explained. Throughout, the concept of confirmation has been emphasized as essential to the proper reading of candlesticks. Among the many forms of confirmation, traditional technical indicators are the best tools you can use.

The Value of Confirmation

For the purpose of using candlesticks as timing tools, perhaps the most important technical concept is *confirmation*. The idea is that no single indicator is reliable, on its own, to clearly and specifically tell you when to enter or exit a position.

No combination of indicators provides a guarantee, either. However, when you see an initial indicator and a confirming one, that increases confidence that the implied meaning is true and correct, whether reversal or confirmation. One aspect of confirmation rarely discussed is the significance of the *lack* of signals. For example, when prices are moving sideways—times in between clear trends when neither buyers nor sellers are in control—the proper indication is to wait on the sidelines until a clear pattern or signal begins to emerge. Thus, the lack of signals itself "confirms" that the proper action is to take no action, but to wait.

Candlestick signs, moves, and patterns provide the strongest possible indicators about the state of a trend. One technical strategy in which confirmation has a particular focus is swing trading. Swing traders rely on the combined indicators found in short-term trends (the clearest candlestick versions of which are three white soldiers or three black crows), narrow-range days (also known as one of the forms of the doji), and volume spikes. These are the three primary indicators and confirmation signals swing traders rely on. However, swing trading would be rudimentary if restricted to only these limited signs. In fact, in a majority of instances, a swing trader will be fortunate to find two of the three signs (trend, NRD, and volume spike) together at the same approximate time. They are fortunate to find two of the three.

In this situation, candlestick analysis enriches the analysis of chart patterns and improves timing of entry and exit. The setups are expanded to dozens of candlestick signs, moves, and patterns, each containing degrees of strength as to what they indicate. Many are clearly bullish or bearish, and some are either, depending on their context on the chart. Because there are so many different candlestick formations, two or more such formations may confirm one another. Some of the preceding chapters provided chart examples showing consecutive candlestick formations in which both pointed to reversal.

Candlestick indicators are further confirmed by noncandlestick signs, notably volume spikes along with candlesticks, especially when reversal is anticipated. Gaps also serve as a very important price trend, and some gaps are invisible. To appreciate the complete meaning of gaps, you need to spot the spaces not only between real bodies from day to day, but also between one day's closing price and the next day's opening price. Even though the ranges overlap, a gap may often be found between days, which may confirm continuation or reversal, depending on what else has appeared on the chart.

Other important signs include some very strong technical indicators, such as the Chaikin Money Flow (CMF) often referred to in previous chapters. It is not only the question of CMF status or direction as a confirming signal, but the strength or weakness of the indicator. Relative status of CMF is a strong indicator on its own. For example, as a continuation indicator during a bull trend, you may note that CMF dips below the line into negative territory. However, if it does not remain there for very long, that indicator tells you that the existing trend is likely to continue.

Additional technical indicators are provided in this chapter. However, before proceeding, we need to emphasize one of the most important of these indicators: the trendline. Remember, the *trend* is the direction of price, and the *trendline* is an indicator that tells you when the trend is beginning to weaken. You can confirm continuation of a trend in many ways, including candlesticks, volume, moving averages, and other technical indicators. However, the trendline is one of the early warning signs. It is drawn under an uptrend and tracks rising support; or above a downtrend, tracking declining resistance.

When the straight line of the trendline begins to fail, it is highly likely that the trend will stop and perhaps reverse in the near future. In numerous examples of charts under analysis, you will find this to be true time and again. As with all indicators, nothing is guaranteed, but trendline study is one of the most reliable confirming indicators, especially when a reverse is also signaled in the candlesticks.

Any confirming indicator takes on additional value when it appears in a set of two—or even three—additional signs. In other words, when you see a candlestick formation that indicates reversal, finding a single confirming sign is encouraging. When you find two or more confirming signs, it is even better. You should not rely solely on candlesticks (or on any other technical indicators) as your only method for entry or exit timing. Candlesticks are the foundation for a timing program, but they need to be confirmed before taking action. The quality, consistency, and reliability of the indicators you use to time your trading decisions will not ensure completely accurate results in every case. You will never get 100 percent of your trades pegged to the perfect entry or exit, but you will improve your rate of well-timed decisions when you rely on confirmation.

A Review: Technical Analysis Basics

The patterns you recognize on charts often help you anticipate what will occur next. Merely the patterns are not enough, however. It is not enough to simplify the process by expecting price to reverse just because it has continued in one direction for several weeks, for example. You need to be able to recognize signals in the candlesticks and combinations of candlestick days, in volume spikes, in a weakening of trendlines, and in well-known tests of resistance and support.

Technical analysis is intended as a means for improving entry and exit timing. This improvement requires the ability to move in and out of positions rapidly and often. For this reason, a widespread belief that technicians are speculators pursuing high-risk trading strategies is not always justified. In fact, proper application of candlestick analysis with a range of confirmation methods can lead to the development of a *conservative* trading strategy. As contradictory as this strategy might seem, it could make more sense than the more traditional buy-and-hold strategy used by value investors.

As the trading cycle becomes more rapid, average holding periods of long positions have been shrinking in recent years. This does not mean that investors are becoming less risk averse; however, it does mean that with improved information and technical systems, higher-volume trading is becoming recognized as a viable alternative to simply buying and holding stock. Figure 10-1 summarizes the average holding period of stock between 1920 and 2009. The period peaked in 1942 at ten years; more recently, the average holding period has declined to below one year.

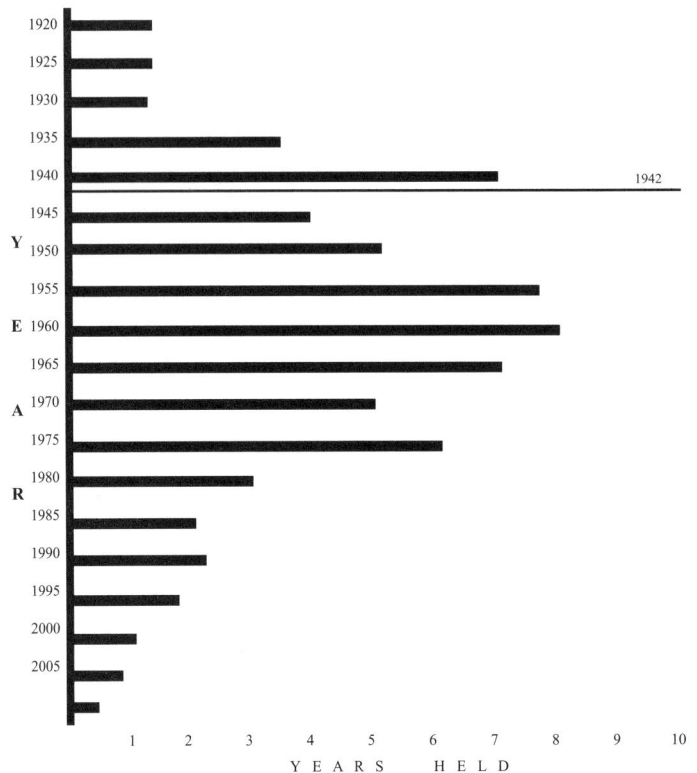

Figure 10-1 Average holding period in years—stocks sold on the New York Stock Exchange

The change makes sense. For example, you will be better off moving in and out of positions as a swing trader if a stock continues trading in a four-point range over 12 months than you would be to just buy shares and wait. As a swing trader, you have several technical advantages:

1. You can earn numerous short-term profits.
2. Potential losses are limited to what may be a relatively small investment level for each swing trade.
3. The activity can be spread or moved among many stocks, which is quite difficult for round lot stock buyers whose available capital is limited.

The purpose of technical analysis is not to guarantee 100 percent success, but to improve your odds of accurately timed entry and exit—based on recognized signals and confirmation within the price movement and its strength or weakness.

Technical analysis is not magic and does not offer a secret formula for success. However, within the broad classification of technical analysis, you will find many "indicators" that have no practical application to price cause and effect. Some indicators are just coincidence. For example, you may not expect to profit by making trading decisions based on the width of annual tree rings, winners of annual sports championships, four-year presidential winners, or even approval ratings. This analysis is controversial, however, because many nonmarket factors such as political policies directly affect the economy. However, the controversy is whether or not you can safely rely on esoteric indicators. If you are willing to perform the hard work of analysis, you can master a few technical basics, including candlestick formations, and apply them to timing decisions.

The best forms of analysis simply make sense and are easily understood. The use of indirect social or political trends is not consistently reliable, and neither are some exceptionally complex technical formulae. Many forms of technical analysis are more academic than practical, so it makes sense to distinguish between working chart studies versus complex mathematical calculations and long-term analysis. Price movement is always going to rely on short-term factors pegged to supply and demand and economic news of the moment. Academic analysis takes solace in long-term averages and statistical likelihood of what will happen next, but realistically, price movement is always chaotic. A long-term statistical study may accurately indicate long-term *future* price movement but cannot be relied on to estimate price direction in the next five days. For that, you need to rely on the technical analysis that is involved directly with price trends.

Technical analysis is not simply the study of where price is and how strong or weak the trend's momentum is at the moment. On a more important level, this analysis helps you to quantify risk. In times of exceptional volatility, a stock's price might exhibit nothing except unpredictability. This behavior, by itself, is a valuable indicator because it cautions you to stay away until more specific trends can be established and acted on. When a trendline moves strongly in one direction but then falters, it could signal reversal; when confirmed by what the candlestick formations tell you, this process reduces risk by giving you the means for timely entry or exit before the reversal occurs.

The Significance of Gaps

Past chapters referred often to gaps as confirming signals for a conclusion based on movement in candlesticks, support and resistance, and trendlines. Gaps are among the most important of technical indicators because they represent a departure from the orderly trading of shares of stock between trading sessions. Incidentally, this general observation applies to the most commonly used trading session period of a trading day, but it applies equally to sessions of any duration—including weekly, hourly, or even five-minute trading sessions. The advantage of observing specific patterns in trades (such as gaps) is that you can apply the meaning of those patterns to any trading duration.

Gaps have a number of different meanings. A gap may be simply a common occurrence within price change from one day to the next. It may be part of a breakout above resistance or below support. There are four specific types of gaps:

1. *Common gap.* This gap is common and easily found. It has no special significance until common gaps begin to appear one after another as part of a developing trend.

📖 Common Gap

A commonly occurring gap in price between one day's close and another day's open, which by itself has no special significance.

2. *Breakaway gap.* This gap has significance, signaling a departure from the established trading range; price moves above resistance or below support with a gap in price.

📖 Breakaway Gap

A gap in price that takes the price range above established resistance or below established support.

3. *Runaway gap.* This type is a gap or series of gaps occurring during a strong and rapid trend.

📖 Runaway Gap

A gap or series of gaps appearing as part of a strong and fast-moving trend.

4. *Exhaustion gap.* A gap appearing at or near the end of a trend, signaling that the price direction is overextended and is about to stop or reverse and fill.

Exhaustion Gap

A gap showing up at or near the end of a trend, signaling an impending reversal to fill the overextended price run.

The quarterly chart of Apple Computer (AAPL), shown in Figure 10-2, provides examples of all four types of gaps. During the period when price levels were trading within the established range, a series of common gaps appeared. The signal of a change in the existing resistance level was marked by the breakaway gap after the doji day. The uptrend that followed was characterized by a series of runaway gaps during a 30-point uptrend in only one month. A two-part exhaustion was signaled by two gaps toward the end of the chart. (This pattern was followed by a one-month period of sideways price movement before price once again went into uptrend mode.)

Chart courtesy of StockCharts.com

Figure 10-2 Gaps

The exhaustion indicator in this case did not precede a downward price movement, but it did signal the end of the run-up because a sideways period followed. The two-part exhaustion gap pattern is also a bullish candlestick pattern: the upside tasuki gap (white day, gap, second white day, and a black third day). This pattern could be interpreted as a signal that, in fact, the uptrend is not ending, only pausing. That interpretation would have been correct. Figure 10-3 extends the Apple chart to show what happened next.

Figure 10-3   Continuation after exhaustion gap

This extended chart is valuable because it demonstrates how the previous exhaustion gap is properly interpreted. It is easy to assume that exhaustion always signals reversal; it may also signal consolidation, as it did in this case. You may have spotted the difference in the fact that the exhaustion gap was a part of the upside tasuki gap pattern. That is a bullish pattern telling you that the current support level is going to hold. This proved to be the case, with support at approximately $160. This was tested on August 17 during the one-month price consolidation. Note the breakaway gap during the newly set trendline, and the very large exhaustion gap in the last week of November. This preceded yet another period of sideways movement in the range of $190 (support) and $205 (resistance). At the end of the chart, a series of small runaway gaps led to a long white candlestick that moved prices above resistance.

These two charts of Apple demonstrate the role that different kinds of gaps play in conjunction with candlestick formations to properly identify the trend. The initial exhaustion gap did not signal reversal because it quickly developed into the upside tasuki. This was not a contradiction; it implied coming sideways movement. The reads of these gaps and candlesticks made it quite possible to properly read the chart even during this volatile period.

A Key Framework: Support and Resistance

Gaps often signal changes in the existing trading range. This range, bordered on the top by resistance and on the bottom by support, is the foundation of technical analysis. It adds a sense of order to how price trends are read. You expect short-term trends to remain inside the borders for a period of time, even if that occurs only so that buyers and sellers can determine what should happen next. In any technical test of trading range limits, the need for confirmation is greater than ever because several possible outcomes may occur.

The argument is that observing the trading range and how support and resistance are tested is not enough analysis to know how to proceed. Some tests of the range lead to breakouts, whereas other breakout moves fail and retreat. How do you know which is taking place as breakout occurs? You cannot know just by virtue of the breakout. This is where candlestick patterns are helpful. The confirmation you obtain by observing breakouts, gaps, tests of support or resistance, and candlestick formations helps in determining whether one of the two events—failed breakout or successful breakout—is most likely to occur. These possible outcomes occur frequently, and both can be confirmed by candlestick formations:

1. *Attempts at breakout fail.* When well-known patterns such as double or triple tops (or bottoms) or head and shoulders form, they often precede strong price movement in the opposite direction. That may also mean a breakaway from the failed breakout attempt. Thus, prices move upward after failing to break through support or move downward after failed tests of resistance.

   An example of a stock whose trading range was tested without successful breakouts was Procter & Gamble (PG), as shown in Figure 10-4. Several interesting patterns emerged here. First was the very prominent hammer at June 22 with the exceptionally long tail. Recall that hammers and hanging man patterns have significance depending on where they appear in a trend. In this case, the hammer showed up immediately after prices fell below support. The long lower shadow tells you that attempts to bring down prices further failed, so you would expect prices to rise again.

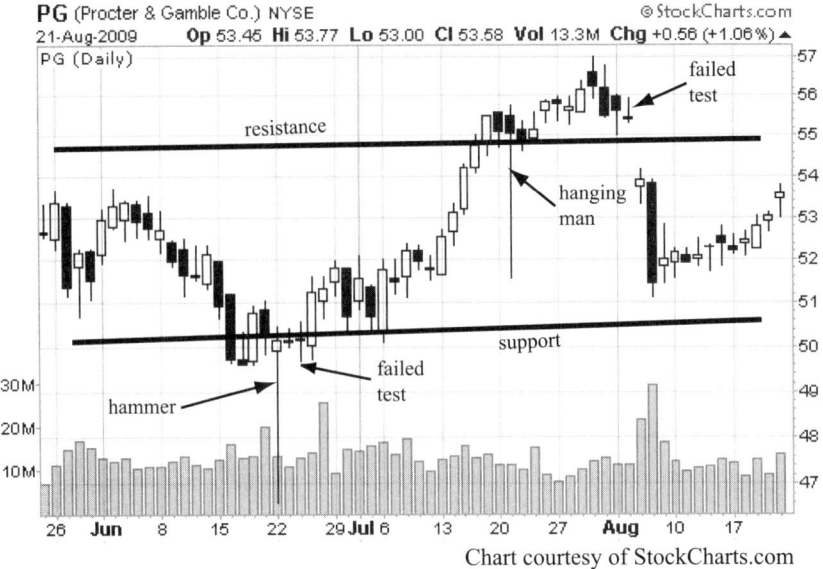

Figure 10-4 Trading range tests with failed breakout

A second occurrence of this pattern recurs at the top, where the same pattern is properly called the hanging man. It showed up immediately after prices rose through resistance and, again, the attempt to bring down prices failed. However, the large gap at the end of the attempted breakout takes prices back into the trading range.

2. *Tests become breakouts.* If prices move strongly away from the trading range, a breakout may occur in the opposite direction. Although a breakout can occur unexpectedly due to indicators beyond price patterns, a predictable event includes the failed test of the opposite border. So a failed double bottom may precede an upside breakout, and vice versa.

The chart of Pfizer (PFE) contained an example of a breakout. A well-established trading range was tested with a double bottom, as shown in Figure 10-5. Immediately after the failed breakout below support, prices began moving upward strongly. After the second test of the bottom, a long white candlestick appeared, starting the upward price movement. At the point of breakout, two consecutive gapping days appeared. First was the change between the black day closing at about 14.75 and the next day opening at about 14.90. The second, larger gap occurred on the next session, which led immediately to the breakout. A new support level was set immediately and held.

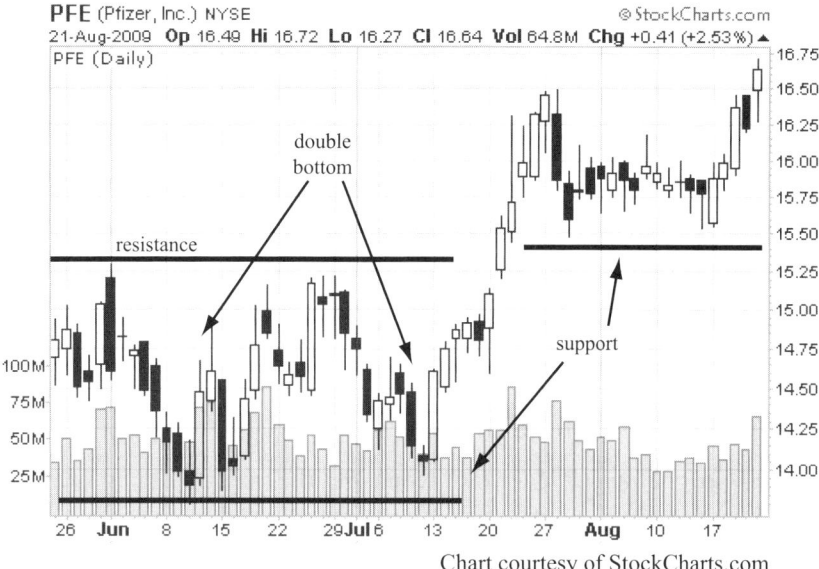

Figure 10-5 Trading range test with successful breakout

Traditional trading range testing patterns, specifically double tops and bottoms or the well-known head-and-shoulders formation, provide very strong early warning signs. However, the appearance of these patterns does not always mean a breakout is going to occur in the opposite direction. It could mean simply that the price range will remain within existing borders and that the failed test merely strengthens support (at the bottom) or resistance (at the top)

On the other side of the breakout, you cannot always rely on its staying power. Some breakouts will set new trading ranges and hold, but many others will fail and prices retreat. Here again, the candlestick confirmation of either event improves your ability to know which event is most likely to follow.

Overbought and Oversold Indicators

Virtually every chartist or technical trader recognizes the more popular price patterns, including those that test support or resistance, trendlines and their conclusion, and price gaps. These easily recognized price changes are strongly confirmed (or contradicted) by observations of candlestick signs, moves, and patterns. You can augment your analysis even further by combining candlestick analysis with even more advanced indicators that calculate whether the current stock price is overbought or oversold.

These indicators are often mathematically intensive, so that in the past your ability to make use of them was limited. Today, however, automated chart generation provides you with instant availability of valuable advanced indicators. In past chapters, some of them were introduced and demonstrated as valuable for confirming trends. The on-balance volume, CMF, and moving average indicators are easily comprehended and work well with traditional technical price patterns and candlesticks. In addition, three technical indicators are worth following because they define whether stocks are overbought or oversold. These three are relative strength index, stochastics, and Bollinger bands.

Relative Strength Index

The *relative strength index (RSI)* compares the strength of uptrend days to that of downtrend days. It often leads the price trend and is especially valuable when other technical indicators do not clearly define the direction of impending price changes.

Relative Strength Index (RSI)

A momentum oscillator that compares the strength of uptrend and downtrend days, and expresses the value on an index between 1 and 100.

The RSI is expressed on an index of 100 and is one of the most reliable of the *momentum oscillators*. This combined terminology refers to the trend direction (momentum) combined with the quantified value (index value) of RSI.

Momentum Oscillator

An indicator such as RSI, expressing a quantified dominance of the trend direction (momentum) on an index (oscillator).

The RSI provides a single index value telling you whether a stock is currently *overbought* or *oversold*. The RSI standard, first introduced by J. Welles Wilder in his 1978 book *New Concepts in Technical Trading Systems*, identifies the RSI level of 70 as overbought and 30 as oversold. This simplified valuation of the stock's condition makes the RSI an exceptionally easy-to-use technical indicator.

📖 Overbought/Oversold

The quantified status of a stock identified through the RSI value as overbought above 70 or as oversold below 30.

To calculate RSI, you add together both upward and downward price changes over a number of sessions (normally 14) and then average them. Next, you divide the up-day average by the down-day average. The result is multiplied by 100 to find the RSI value. However, you do not need to go through the tedium of making these calculations yourself because many online sites provide free stock charts with RSI included.

Stochastics

The next advanced technical indicator is called *stochastics*. This is a *price oscillator*, which is a calculation of the differences between two moving averages. However, whereas *MACD* is invariably based on the exponential moving averages of 12 and 26 sessions, the price oscillator provides a percentage difference that shifts between positive and negative.

📖 Stochastics

A momentum indicator identifying current price in relationship to the current trading range; the word means "random" and is a means for calculating the likely price movement in the near future.

📖 Price Oscillator

A technical indicator based on comparisons between two moving averages.

📖 MACD

The moving average convergence/divergence, a technical calculation comparing the trend between two fixed moving averages.

You calculate the stochastics formula by comparing changes in longer-term moving average and shorter-term moving average. This produces a point-based outcome. To convert to a percentage-based outcome, you multiply the result by 100. As with other advanced technical indicators, stochastics outcomes are plotted automatically on many web-based free charting services.

Just as RSI defines overbought and oversold as residing above 70 and below 30, the stochastics version is similar, with overbought levels usually identified as 80 and oversold at 20.

Bollinger Bands

The third overbought/oversold indicator is called *Bollinger bands*, named after the technician John Bollinger who introduced the concept in the 1980s. The method begins with a calculation of a moving average over a specified period of time. (Bollinger recommended using 20 days.) The next step applies the statistical calculation known as standard deviation to quantify the "highness" or "lowness" of price in relation to previous price levels. This produces bands running above and below the moving average. The distance between the average and the bands measures volatility.

📖 Bollinger Bands

A technical indicator that tracks the relative distance of current price from a moving average, visually displaying price volatility levels.

Combined with RSI and stochastics, Bollinger bands prominently define overbought and oversold conditions. Volatility levels are highly visible with the upper and lower bands easily compared to current price levels.

All three of these indicators can be studied together to provide technical confirmation; when used in conjunction with traditional chart patterns and candlesticks, they round out your program of technical analysis. For example, the six-month chart of Gold Trust Shares (GLD), in Figure 10-6, shows price with Bollinger bands and moving average behind, and RSI and stochastics indicators below.

The Bollinger bands track price with variations indicating varying levels of volatility; these variations tend to grow as the trendline continues. Note how the lower band bounces from the trendline, below, and then back. Meanwhile, the upper bands follow the price levels very closely. This pattern continues until the price peaks near $119. The run-up in price was characterized by numerous runaway gaps and then two exhaustion gaps at the top. Also note how the trendline ends abruptly as price begins to decline.

Figure 10-6 Overbought/oversold indicators

These conditions were confirmed in several ways. The RSI remained mostly between the 70 and 30 percentiles, indicating that prices were reasonable. This continued until the period when condition became overbought, rising at one point to about 85. As price retreated, RSI levels also fell back into the middle zone.

The stochastics line contradicted RSI in many respects, providing many instances where the line showed overbought conditions, as the trendline and price rose quickly. Although RSI reported price at reasonable levels toward the conclusion of the chart, stochastics fell well below the 20 percent level, indicating that the decline to about $105 was an oversold price level.

The trendline confirmed the overbought/oversold indicators and Bollinger volatility. However, the real confirmation is found in the candlesticks. In the early part of October, note the short-term uptrend with a strong price gap moving through the short-term resistance level. A second rally occurred in early November with a gap and then a long white candle. The marked runaway and exhaustion gaps confirm the overbought conditions confirmed by both RSI and stochastics. As the price reached its highest level, it was followed immediately by a doji, downward gap, and long black candlestick. All these predicted a downturn, confirmed when price met and fell below the trendline. Stochastics confirmed this behavior, although RSI did not.

This chart provides a lot of information, but it is not consistent. This example shows why you need to use several different indicators. In this example, RSI pegged the overbought condition but did not agree with the stochastics when it identified the following low point as oversold. Although employing a large number of indicators will result in varying levels of disagreement as to what the indicators reveal, this level of analysis is quite reasonable. There is enough at the top of the trend to accurately predict reversal: exhaustion gaps, black candlesticks, and both RSI and stochastics overbought range movements. The resulting conclusions about the downtrend and whether or not the stock became oversold is not agreed on; the RSI in particular indicates that the price range is fair, whereas stochastics plunged below 20.

The Potential of Candlestick Signals

No indicators or combination of indicators provides a guarantee that the signals are always reliable. By the same argument, no candlestick formations can provide assurance that entry and exit timing will be flawless. All these indicators, when used to confirm one another or to provide agreement on the continuation or reversal of a trend, will improve the instances of well-timed trading decisions.

The possibility of false signals is ever present. With this point in mind, it is imperative that you view candlesticks as one of many tests. The candlestick signs, moves, and patterns presented in this book and shown in the context of reversal and continuation are probably more accurate as predictive indicators than most other forms of price analysis. However, as dozens of past examples have shown, *confirmation* is the necessary attribute to a sensible program of technical analysis. Different candlestick formations may confirm one another when they appear side by side; and indicators other than candlesticks, including moving averages, trendlines, volume, and advanced technical indices, aid in the development of an accurate and reliable system.

A lot of emphasis has been placed not only on confirmation, but also on the possibility that even the strongest indicator may be false—even when confirmed by any number of other indicators. No trader should expect to rely on a timing system to the extent that risks become higher than acceptable. Remember, the purpose of all these indicator studies is not to completely eliminate risk, but to reduce it. In the process, an improved and more reliable system is designed to increase the success of your timing. If you use only a single indicator, you may expect a 50 percent accuracy rate, for example. However, by combining a singular analytical system with a series of confirming signals, you may expect to realize a much higher degree of success.

Candlestick analysis involves dozens of potential formations, and each has its own degree of significance. Some are bullish, others bearish; some indicate coming reversal, others tell you continuation is more likely. A few contain significance that depends on position within a trend (for example, appearing at the conclusion of an uptrend versus a downtrend). With these points in mind, you cannot oversimplify candlestick analysis or expect it to always provide an identical conclusion. That relies on the momentum of the trend, confirmation in many forms, and acceptance of the reality that even the strongest predictive indicator will be wrong sometimes.

The "right or wrong" of a decision is not determined by the degree of accuracy in how you read the signals. It is a percentage of well-timed decisions, and using candlesticks for the purpose of increasing this percentage is where your real advantage lies. In that sense, candlestick analysis is not an absolute science. However, it is effective at improving the quality of the estimate involved in your timing decisions. To a degree, all trading decisions involve part guesswork. Candlestick analysis is a method for improving the success of the guesses you need to make.

appendix

Glossary

Accumulation/distribution (AD): A technical indicator measuring proportionate degrees of buyer and seller volume; it acts as a momentum indicator.
Ascending triangle: A bullish triangle characterized by a level resistance and rising support level.
Bear abandoned baby: A complex formation consisting of a bear *doji* star (an upward day, an upward gap, and a *doji*) followed by a downward gap and then a downward day.
Bear squeeze alert: A three-session candle with the first one upward, the second with a narrower opening and closing range, and the third with yet narrower ranges. Although second and third session candles may be upward or downward, the strongest version of the squeeze alert contains three white candles.
Belt hold: A reversal pattern consisting of three downtrend days, a downside gap, and a white candle with no lower shadow (bull); or three uptrend days, an upside gap, and a black candle with no upper shadow (bear).
Bollinger bands: A technical indicator that tracks the relative distance of current price from a moving average, visually displaying price volatility levels.
Breakaway gap: A gap in price that takes the price range above established resistance or below established support.
Breakaway pattern: A reversal pattern in which the first candle is followed by a gap in the direction established (downward for a black candle or upward for a white candle). A series of the same-colored candles follows moving in the same direction, concluding with a candle of the opposite color closing into the gap (upward for a bull breakaway or downward for a bear breakaway).

Bull abandoned baby: A complex pattern consisting of a bull *doji* star (a downward day, downward gap, and *doji*) followed by an upward gap and then an upward day.

Bull squeeze alert: A three-session candle with the first one downward, the second with a narrower opening and closing range, and the third with yet narrower ranges. Although the second and third session candles may be upward or downward, the strongest version of the squeeze alert contains three black candles.

Candlestick chart: A visual summary of all the trading action in a single period, showing the opening and closing prices, breadth of trading, and upward or downward movement in price.

Coil: Alternate name for the symmetrical triangle.

Common gap: A commonly occurring gap in price between one day's close and another day's open, which by itself has no special significance.

Complex patterns: Candlestick formations consisting of three or more consecutive trading sessions and creating one of several specific reversal or directional indicators.

Concealing baby swallow: A bull reversal pattern consisting of four black candles; the first two are *marubozus*, followed by a downside gap, a third black candle, and then an engulfing black candle. This pattern sets a new support level for the trading range.

Confirmation: The use of an indicator to verify the meaning of a separate indicator occurring at the same time or earlier, consisting of movement in an index or individual stock price, changes in price trend direction, or initiation of an entry or existing signal.

Confirming indicators: Candlestick formations that anticipate that the current trend is likely to continue in the same direction.

Consolidation: A period in which a narrow trading range is in effect and little if any movement occurs. It is likely to occur in between upward or downward trends and reflects uncertainty in the market about future price direction.

Contrarian investor: A trader or investor who recognizes that markets overreact to news and who makes buy and sell decisions in a direction opposite the prevailing trend.

Convergence/divergence: The tendency for two long-term moving averages of price to move toward one another (converge) or away from one another (diverge).

Dark cloud cover: Alternate name for the bear piercing lines move.

Descending triangle: A bearish continuation pattern consisting of steady support price and declining resistance.

Doji: A candlestick sign developed when the day's opening and closing prices are identical or very close; the real body is a horizontal line rather than a box.

Doji star: A variation of the inverted hammer in which the signal day forms as a *doji* instead of a hammer candle.

Downside gap filled: A bear complex pattern with a downward session, a downside gap, a second downside session, and then a third session moving to the upside. However, although the third session fills the gap, it does not move above the resistance level set by the first day's opening price.

Downside *tasuki* gap: A complex pattern creating a bear trend with a downward candle, a downside gap, a second downward candle, and then an upside candle that does not fill the gap. It is a bear formation because the gap holds up.

Downtrend: A short-term pattern of three or more periods, characterized by each period's lower low price levels and lower high price levels.

Dragonfly *doji*: A type of *doji* with a lower shadow; the longer the shadow, the greater the bullish indication.

Engulfing pattern: A double-stick move in which the range of the setup period's stick is surpassed by the range of the signal period, and in which the setup stick's shadows are longer than those of the signal period.

Evening star: A bear three-stick pattern combining a bear inverted hammer with a subsequent third day moving downward.

Exhaustion gap: A gap showing up at or near the end of a trend, signaling an impending reversal to fill the overextended price run.

Falling three pattern: A bear reversal pattern and the opposite of the bull reversal mat hold. This pattern consists of a black session, a downside gap, a series of rising white sessions, and a final black session closing lower than the close of the first. This pattern sets a new resistance level and anticipates a downtrend.

Falling wedge: A reversal pattern in which prices fall while the price range narrows, anticipating a coming price rise.

Gapping trend: Any trend involving price gaps, especially between trading sessions in which the gaps are not immediately visible.

Gravestone *doji*: A type of *doji* with an upper shadow; the longer the shadow, the greater the bearish indication.

Hammer: A pattern with a small ready body, no upper shadow, and a longer than usual lower shadow. It appears at the bottom of a downtrend and is a bullish day indicating an impending reversal, or it appears as confirmation during an uptrend.

Hanging man: A pattern with a small real body, no upper shadow, and a longer than usual lower shadow. It appears at the top of an uptrend and is a bearish day indicating an impending reversal, or it appears as confirmation during a downtrend.

Harami: Meaning "pregnant," a double-stick move in which the setup day's range is longer than the signal's days, extending above the high and below the low, and when the setup's shadows are longer than those of the stick in the signal period.

Harami **cross:** A type of *harami* in which the signal day forms a *doji* and is subject to the same range requirements of other *harami* moves.

In neck: A variation of the neck line move in which the two days' real bodies overlap somewhat in price levels.

Inside down: A three-stick formation with a bear *harami* in the first two sessions (a white first day and a smaller black second day in a narrower range) and then a third downward day.

Inside up: A three-stick formation with a bull *harami* in the first two sessions (a black first day and a smaller white second day in a narrower range) and then a third upward day.

Inverted hammer: A double-stick move made up of a downward trending long candle, a low-side gap, and a hammer (a bull formation); or an upward moving long candle, a high-side gap, and a hammer (a bear formation).

Kicking: A reversal pattern consisting of a *marubozu*, a gap above or below, and then a candle of the opposite color. A bull kicking starts with a black and ends with a white candle with an upside gap between the two, and a bear kicking starts with a white candle and ends with a black candle with a downside gap between the two.

Ladder pattern: A reversal pattern beginning with a series of candles trending in one direction, a gap in the opposite direction, and a candle that moves in the reversal direction. A ladder bottom (black candles, an upside gap, and a higher white session) is a bull reversal, and a ladder top (white candles, a downside gap, and a black session) is a bear reversal.

Long-legged *doji*: A *doji* sign with exceptionally large upper and lower shadows, indicating a coming reversal in the current trend.

MACD: The moving average convergence/divergence, a technical calculation comparing the trend between two fixed moving averages.

Major yin: A black *marubozu* sign serving as a reversal sign within a downtrend or, when it appears within an uptrend, as a continuation indicator.

Marubozu: A long candlestick, with varying lengths of upper and lower shadows. The word in Japanese means "with little hair."

Mat hold: A bull reversal pattern beginning with a long white candle, followed by an upside gap, downward black candles, and a final white candle closing higher than the first candle.

Glossary

Matching pattern: A bull reversal move consisting of two black candles with identical closing prices (matching low), establishing a new support level; or a bear reversal with two white candles with identical closing prices (matching high), establishing a new resistance level.

Meeting lines: A double-stick move with the bottom of the setup day's real body meeting the top of the real body in the signal day. In a bull move, the setup day is downward moving and the signal day is upward, creating a downward gap between the closing price of the setup and the opening price of the signal. A bear meeting lines move exhibits the opposite direction in both sessions and an upside gap in between.

Momentum oscillator: An indicator such as RSI, expressing a quantified dominance of the trend direction (momentum) on an index (oscillator).

Money flow: A technical test of volume trends employing the average of each day's high, low, and close to develop a cumulative trend direction in price.

Money flow index (MFI): A momentum indicator measuring positive and negative money flow in a stock's price over a 21-day moving average, creating an oscillator ranging between 1 and 100; the indicator is also known as the Chaikin Money Flow (CMF).

Morning star: A bull three-stick pattern combining a bull inverted hammer with a subsequent third day moving upward.

Move: A double-stick formation that foreshadows either a reversal or continuation in the current price trend.

Near-*doji*: A candlestick with an exceptionally thin space between opening and closing prices; although they are not identical, the range is so small that the candle is granted the same significance as a perfect *doji*.

Neck line: A double-stick confirming move with long candlesticks. The setup is upward and a higher signal is downward (bull pattern), or the setup is downward and the signal is upward (bear pattern). In both cases, a gap is closed in the setup day, confirming the current trend.

Northern *doji*: Any doji appearing above a previous uptrend, considered a strong bear signal.

OHLC chart: Abbreviation of "open, high, low, close." A type of stock chart showing a vertical stick for the day's trading range and two vertical, shorter protrusions showing opening and closing prices.

On neck: A variation of the neck line move in which the two days' real bodies intersect at approximately the same price level.

On-balance volume: A cumulative indicator measuring dominance of daily trading by either buyers or sellers, used to anticipate emerging trends.

Outside down: A complex pattern consisting of a bear engulfing (two sticks made up of a white day and then a larger black day with higher high and higher low) and a third day moving lower.

Outside up: A complex pattern consisting of a bull engulfing (two sticks made up of a black day and then a larger white day with higher high and higher low) and a third day moving higher.

Overbought/oversold: The quantified status of a stock identified through the RSI value as overbought above 70 or as oversold below 30.

Paper trading: A method for becoming familiar with strategies, in which a fictitious portfolio is traded using "virtual money." This enables you to see the outcomes of different timing strategies, but without losing real money.

Pattern: A candlestick formation of three or more trading periods that strongly indicates a reversal or continuation of the current trend.

Percentage swing system: A method of timing entry and exit based on the percentage by which price moves above or below the previously establishing trading range.

Piercing lines: A double-stick move with two long candles. A bull formation has a downward movement in the setup and a lower, upward movement in the signal, with trading ranges overlapping to form an invisible gap.

Price oscillator: A technical indicator based on comparisons between two moving averages.

Primary trend: The overall price direction in the market, either bull (upward) or bear (downward). Within each primary trend, offsetting secondary trends occur.

Reaction swing: A tendency for short-term prices to return to an established trading range following a price spike.

Real body: The rectangle in a candlestick, representing the area between the day's opening and closing price but excluding the total range above and below those levels (upper and lower shadows).

Relative strength index (RSI): A momentum oscillator that compares the strength of uptrend and downtrend days, and expresses the value on an index between 1 and 100.

Reversal formations: Candlestick developments signaling the end of the current trend and anticipating the likelihood that price will next move in the opposite direction.

Reversion to the mean: A tendency for prices to reverse course and move back toward their longer-term average.

Rising wedge: A reversal pattern in which prices rise while the price range narrows, anticipating a coming price decline.

Risk tolerance: The degree of risk you are willing and able to take in your portfolio, based on many factors, including knowledge about the market, experience, capital, budget, portfolio size, and personal financial situation. The defined risk tolerance level identifies the kinds of investments anyone can afford to make.

Runaway gap: A gap or series of gaps appearing as part of a strong and fast-moving trend.

Separating lines: A confirming double-stick move creating a gap equal to the real body of the setup day. A bull formation is formed with a downward setup and a higher upward signal. A bear move is formed with an upward setup and a lower downward signal.

Setup: The first trading period in a multistick formation, followed by the signal trading period.

Shadow: The portion of the candlestick above and below the real body. The upper shadow shows the distance between the trading range (open to close) and the highest price of the day, and the lower shadow shows the distance between the trading range and the lowest price of the day.

Side-by-side black lines bear: A formation of three black sessions. The first is followed by a downside gap and then two additional downward moving sessions.

Side-by-side black lines bull: A formation of one white session, an upside gap, and two black sessions. Price support prevents the bears from moving price down to fill the gap and forms new support, making this a bullish indicator.

Side-by-side white lines bear: A pattern of one black session, an upside gap, and two white sessions. Price resistance prevents the bulls from moving price up to fill the gap, making this a bearish indicator.

Side-by-side white lines bull: A pattern of three white sessions. The first is followed by an upside gap and then two additional upward moving sessions.

Sign: A single candlestick that provides initial indications about a reversal or continuation in the overall trend.

Signal: The last trading period in a multistick formation, which occurs after the setup.

Southern *doji*: Any doji appearing below a previous downtrend, considered a strong bull signal.

Spike: A sudden price move above or below the trading range, which often is followed by a return to that range within a few trading sessions.

Spinning top: A candlestick with a relatively small real body and upper and lower shadows. The real body is approximately midway in the day's range, and both shadows are at least the same size as the real body.

Stick sandwich: A reversal three-stick pattern in which the first and third sticks are one color; and the middle, the opposite color. The closing prices of the first and third sticks are at the same level, establishing new support (bull) or new resistance (bear) price levels.

Stochastics: A momentum indicator identifying current price in relationship to the current trading range; the word means "random" and is a means for calculating the likely price movement in the near future.

Swing trade: A trade with a short time in a position, entered after price spikes or percentages above the norm of movement; the purpose is to time short-term profits by trading contrary to the market tendency.

Symmetrical triangle: A continuation pattern consisting of a trading range of the same breadth in both the beginning of the triangle and the continuation.

Tails: An alternate term for especially long upper and lower shadows, used as indicators of the degree of strength in bullish or bearish trends.

Three black crows: A complex candlestick formation consisting of three or more consecutive downward candles. Each has a lower opening and a lower closing than the previous candle.

Three rivers pattern: A reversal formation consisting of a long black candle, a lower black candle, and a short white candle closing lower (three rivers bottom, a bull formation); or a long white candle, a higher white candle, and a short black candle closing higher (three rivers top, a bear formation).

Three stars in the south: A bull reversal consisting of three black candles. The first has a long lower shadow, the second closes lower, and the third is a *marubozu* with a range within the range of the second session.

Three white soldiers: A complex candlestick formation consisting of three or more consecutive upward candles. Each has a higher opening and a higher closing than the previous candle.

Thrusting lines: A double-stick confirming move consisting of two long candles. In a bull formation, setup is upward and a higher signal day is downward. In a bear formation, setup is downward and a lower signal day is upward moving.

Total capitalization: The sum of capital that funds a company's operations, consisting of equity (shareholders' capital) and debt (long-term loans and bonds).

Trading range: The price spread between highest and lowest points on a daily bar or over a period of time; the breadth of trading between those two points.

Trend: The direction of price movement over time, which continues in the same movement until it weakens and moves sideways or reverses.

Trendline: A series of straight lines bordering the highest and lowest point in a current price trend.

Triangles: Continuation patterns characterized by a narrowing trading range over time; they may be symmetrical, ascending, or descending.

Tri-star: A pattern with three consecutive sessions showing *dojis* in each. A bull tri-star develops when the middle *doji* gaps below the ranges of the first and third sessions, and a bear tri-star consists of a second session gapping above the first and third.

True range: A stock's trading range within a trend rather than a single trading session. It includes the previous session's closing price and the current session's price movement.

Upside gap filled: A bull complex pattern with an upward session, an upside gap, a second upside session, and then a third session moving to the downside. However, although the third session fills the gap, it does not fall below the support level set by the first day's opening price.

Upside *tasuki* gap: A complex pattern creating a bull trend with an upward candle, an upside gap, a second upward candle, and then a downside candle that does not fill the gap. It is a bull formation because the gap holds up.

Uptrend: A short-term pattern of three or more periods, characterized by each period's higher high price levels and high low price levels.

Wedge: A reversal pattern in one of two shapes: a rising wedge is bearish, anticipating a reversal from the existing uptrend to a downtrend; and a falling wedge is bullish, anticipating a reversal from the existing downtrend to an uptrend.

Index

A

abandoned baby, 78-82
accumulation/distribution (AD), 125-126
Alcoa (AA):
    bearish volume indicator, 129
    bull squeeze alert, 73
    falling wedge, 138-139
    inside down, 76
    marubozu with volume spike, 157-158
    three black crows false reversal, 95
American Express (AXP):
    bullish volume indicator, 127-129
    consolidation with marubozu breakout, 154-155
    engulfing moves, 49
    white soldiers and black crows, 71-72
anticipating the trend, 153-156
Apple (AAPL):
    continuation after exhaustion gap, 214
    exit signals followed by continuation, 188
    gaps, 213
    inside up, 75
    percentage of change system, 147
ascending triangle, 134-135
average holding period, 210

B

Bank of America (BAC):
    ascending triangle, 135
    bull abandoned baby, 80-81
    consolidation with inverse head and shoulders, 155
    meeting lines, 57-58

bear:
    abandoned baby, 81-82
    belt hold, 103
    breakaway, 112-113
    reversal, 94-97
    squeeze alert, 73-74
    stick sandwich, 106-107
bearish volume indicator, 129
belt hold, 102-103
Best Buy (BBY):
    bullish tail, 42-43
    false indicator: marubozu with volume spike, 157-159
    outside up and down, 77
    rising wedge, 137
black crows, 71-72
Boeing (BA):
    bear breakaway, 112-113
    bear inverted hammer, 54
    CMF move with repetitive price gaps, 162-163
    downside gap filled, 89
Bollinger bands, 220
breakaway gap, 212
breakaway pattern, 111-113, 145
bull:
    abandoned baby, 80-81
    belt hold, 102-103
    breakaway, 112
    reversal, 91-96
    squeeze alert, 72-73
    stick sandwich, 105-106

bullish:
    long candlestick, 30-32
    tail, 43
    volume indicator, 127-128

C

candlestick:
    attributes, 8-9
    bullish long, 30-32
    chart, defined, 5
    complex patterns, 69-70
    confirmation, 200-203
    entry or exit, 182-186
    formations, 19
    moving averages, 203-206
    observations of, 18-20
    potential, 222-223
    shapes, 28-30
    strengths and weaknesses, 9-11
    swing trading with, 174-178
    volume indicators and, 126-131
Caterpillar (CAT):
    downward trendline ending, 200-201
    morning star false reversal, 93-94
    moving averages with candlestick trends, 180-181
    price gap with volume spike, 160
Chaikin Money Flow (CMF), 126-131, 153, 157, 162-164, 208
Chevron Corp (CVX):
    bear stick sandwich, 106-107
    false indicator: CMP move with repetitive price gaps, 163-164

Cisco (CSCO):
  bear squeeze alert, 73-74
  breakout with no volume spike, 121-122
Coca-Cola (KO):
  marubozu, 31-32
  neck line move (bull), 64-65
  piercing lines, 59
  trend with marubozu but no breakout, 167-168
coil, 133
common gap, 87, 212
complex trend patterns, 82-85
concealing baby swallow, 104-105
confirmation, 19-20, 200-209
confirming indicators, 60-61
confirming moves, 66-67
consolidation, 153-156
contradictory volume indicator, 130
contrarian investor, 142-143
convergence/divergence, 178-182

D

dark cloud cover, 59
descending triangle, 135-136
Disney (DIS):
  harami, 51
  neck line (bear), 65-66
  tasuki gap, 86-87
  three rivers bottom, 110
dividend yield, 21
doji:
  dragonfly, 33-34
  gravestone, 35
  long-legged, 35-37
  narrow-range day, 32
  near, 98
  northern, 98
  reversal signal, 97-100
  southern, 98
  star, 53-56
  tri-star pattern, 99-100
downside:
  gap filled, 89
  tasuki gap, 86
downtrends, 25-28
dragonfly doji, 33-34
DuPont (DD):
  bear abandoned baby, 81-82
  contradictory volume indicator, 130
  exit signals followed by reversal, 189
  ladder top, 116-117

E

engulfing, 48-52, 76-77
entry signals, 186
evening star, 79-80
exhaustion gap, 213-214
exit signals, 187-189
Exxon-Mobil (XOM):
  bull belt hold, 102-103
  bull breakaway, 112
  dragonfly doji, 33-34
  failing spinning tops, 39
  falling three pattern, 114-115
  multiple reversal signals, 176-177

side-by-side white lines bear, 85
three white soldiers false reversal, 92
trendline in a downtrend, 199

F

falling three pattern, 114-115
falling wedge, 138-139
fundamental volatility, 132

G

gap:
    breakaway, 212-213
    common, 87, 212-213
    complex 86-90
    exhaustion, 213-214
    filled, 87-88
    multisession reversals, 111-117
    repetitive, 162-164
    reversal patterns with, 101-104
    runaway, 212-213
    short-term behavior, 149-153
    significance of, 212-215
    tasuki, 86-87
    trend, 150-152
    with volume spike, 160-162
    without breakout, 168-169
General Electric (GE):
    harami cross, 52
    northern and southern dojis, 99
Gold Trust Shares (GLD),
    overbought/oversold indicators, 220-221
Google (GOOG):
    bear belt hold, 103
    ladder bottom, 116
    spinning top, 37-38
gravestone doji, 35

H

hammer, 37-41, 79
hanging man, 37-41
harami, 48-52, 74-75, 167
harami cross, 51-52
Hewlett-Packard (HPQ):
    percentage of change system, 148-149
    trendline in an uptrend, 198
Home Depot (HD) upside gap filled, 88

I

in neck, 64-66
information pool, 20-22
inside formations, 74-77
Intel (INTC):
    evening star, 79-80
    spike with breakaway and new range, 144-145
inverse head and shoulders, 155
inverted hammer, 53-56

J

JCPenney (JCP):
    bull stick sandwich, 106
    dragonfly doji failure, 34-35

hammer, 40-41
three rivers top, 111
Johnson & Johnson (JNJ):
    bull side-by-side black lines, 84
    evening star false reversal, 96
    moving averages to support trends, 203-204

K

kicking, 101-102
Kraft Foods (KFT):
    false indicator: price gap with volume spike, 161
    short-term trends within the primary trend, 183

L

ladder pattern, 115-117
long-legged doji, 35-37

M

MACD (moving average convergence/divergence), 219
major yin, 124
marubozu, 30-32, 124, 128, 154-160, 166-168
mat hold, 113-114
matching pattern, 107-108
McDonald's (MCD):
    bull inverted hammer, 53
    concealing baby swallow, 104-105
    gapping trend, 152
    hanging man, 39-40
    morning star, 78-79
    upward trendline ending, 201-202
meeting lines, 56-60
Merck (MRK):
    price direction confirmed within a primary trend, 185
    short-term trends with strong candlestick signals, 183-184
Microsoft (MSFT):
    symmetrical triangle, 133-134
    trend with gaps but no breakout, 168-169
mistake pattern, 32-37
MMM (3M Co.), volume as a leading indicator, 123-124
momentum oscillator, 218
money flow index (MFI), 125
morning star, 78-79
moving average (MA), 179-181, 203-206

N

narrow-range day (NRD), 32, 38, 145, 189
near doji, 98
neck lines, 60-66
nonrecurring price spike, 143-144
northern doji, 98

O

OHLC (open, high, low, close) chart, 7-10, 29
on neck, 64-66
on-balance volume, 124-125
outside formations, 74-77
overbought and oversold conditions, 217-222

P-Q

P/E (price/earnings) ratio, 21, 132
paper trading, 12-14
percentage swing systems, 146-150
Pfizer (PFE):
    mat hold, 113-114
    price breakout following marubozu, 166
    separating lines, 63
    trading range test with successful breakout, 216-217
piercing lines, 56-60
price oscillator, 219
price spikes, 143-146
primary trend, 178-179, 182-186
Procter & Gamble (PG):
    nonrecurring price spike, 143-144
    trading range tests with failed breakout, 215-216

R

reaction swings, 143-146
real body, 9
relative strength index (RSI), 218

resistance:
    key framework, 215-217
    reversals and, 104-111
    swing trade, 165-169
reversal:
    formations, defined, 47
    multisession gap, 111-117
    patterns with gaps, 101-104
    stars, 78-82
    support and resistance, 104-111
    trend change patterns, 71-74
reversion to the mean, 194-195
rising wedge, 137-138
risk tolerance, 14
runaway gap, 212

S

selling short, 190-192
separating lines, 60-66
setup, 48, 156-164, 186-190
shadow, 9
short-term gapping behavior, 149-153
side-by-side lines, 82-85
signal session, 48
southern doji, 98
spike, 143
spinning top, 37-41
squeeze alert, 72-74
stick sandwich, 105-106
stochastics, 219

support:
    key framework, 215-217
    reversals and, 104-111
    swing trade, 165-169
swing trade:
    defined, 141-142
    overview, 171-174
    price movement, 174-178
    setup pattern, 165-169
    short selling, 190-192
symmetrical triangle, 133-134

T

tails, 42-45
tasuki gaps, 86-87
technical analysis, 209-211
testing price volatility, 131-139
three rivers pattern, 110
three stars in the south, 109
thrusting lines, 60-66
total capitalization, 21
trading range, defined, 7
trading skills, 14-18
Travelers (TRV):
    retreating volume trend, 121
    uptrends and downtrends, 27-28
trend, defined, 6
trendline:
    candlestick confirmation, 200-203
    defined, 193-194, 197-198
    identification, 194-200

triangles, 133-136
tri-star pattern, 99-100
true range, 149-150

U

United Technologies (UTX):
    doji star, 55-56
    matching moves, 107-108
upside gap filled, 87-88
upside tasuki gap, 86
uptrends, 25-28

V

Verizon (VZ):
    ascending triangle, 135-136
    side-by-side lines, 83
volume as price indicator, 119-122

W-X

Wal-Mart (WMT):
    long-legged doji, 36
    price breakout following bullish harami, 167
    thrusting lines, 61-62
wedge, 136-139
white soldiers, 71-72

Y-Z

Yahoo! (YHOO):
    gapping trend, 151
    multiple reversal signals, 175-176
    three stars in the south, 109

In an increasingly competitive world, it is quality of thinking that gives an edge—an idea that opens new doors, a technique that solves a problem, or an insight that simply helps make sense of it all.

We work with leading authors in the various arenas of business and finance to bring cutting-edge thinking and best-learning practices to a global market.

It is our goal to create world-class print publications and electronic products that give readers knowledge and understanding that can then be applied, whether studying or at work.

To find out more about our business products, you can visit us at www.ftpress.com.